AMERICAN
POWER

AMERICAN POWER

POTENTIAL AND LIMITS
IN THE 21st CENTURY

EDITED BY

PATRICK LUCIANI &
RUDYARD GRIFFITHS

THE GRANO SPEAKER'S SERIES
2004–2006

KEY PORTER BOOKS

Library and Archives Canada Cataloguing in Publication

American power : potential and limits in the twenty-first century / Patrick Luciani and
Rudyard Griffiths, general editors.

ISBN-13: 978-1-55263-909-2, ISBN-10: 1-55263-909-6

1. United States—Foreign relations—Middle East. 2. Middle East—Foreign relations—United
States. 3. United States—Foreign relations—2001-. I. Luciani, Patrick II. Griffiths, Rudyard

DS63.2.U5A64 2007   327.73056'09'0511   C2007-901840-8

ONTARIO ARTS COUNCIL
CONSEIL DES ARTS DE L'ONTARIC

The publisher gratefully acknowledges the support of the Canada Council for the Arts and
the Ontario Arts Council for its publishing program. We acknowledge the support of the
Government of Ontario through the Ontario Media Development Corporation's Ontario
Book Initiative.

We acknowledge the financial support of the Government of Canada through the Book
Publishing Industry Development Program (BPIDP) for our publishing activities.

Key Porter Books Limited
Six Adelaide Street East, Tenth Floor
Toronto, Ontario
Canada M5C 1H6

www.keyporter.com

Text design: Marijke Friesen
Electronic formatting: Jean Lightfoot Peters

Printed and bound in Canada

07 08 09 10 11 5 4 3 2 1

CONTENTS

ACKNOWLEDGMENTS

The Grano Speakers Series would never have succeeded without the help of our sponsors. When we first proposed the idea to our patrons—industrialist Peter Munk, former Canadian ambassador to the United States Allan Gotlieb, and philanthropists Sandra and Joseph Rotman—they not only enthusiastically supported our venture financially through their foundations, they played a crucial role with their advice and guidance. We also want to acknowledge the support of the Honorable Hilary Weston and Galen Weston, Hugh Mackinnon of Bennett Jones and Richard Rooney of Burgundy Financial. Other supporters of the series include Tridel Developers, the Donner Canadian Foundation, the Black Family Foundation, the Atlantic Institute for Market Studies, Gluskin Sheff, Minto Developers and our wine supplier, Vince Liberatore.

Event organizer Carla Martella kept the whole thing going as each event approached. Special thanks also go to the former editor of the *Toronto Star* Giles Gherson, who made it possible to reach a broad audience, and Legal Transcripts who did an excellent job with all lecture transcriptions. At Key Porter, our publisher, we are especially grateful to Linda Pruessen for encouraging and keeping the book on track and on time.

We particularly want to thank Roberto and Lucia Martella—owners and proprietors of Grano, and perfect hosts to the series—for so generously opening up their restaurant and guaranteeing the success of the series. Grano turned out to be an ideal venue for the series. Grano isn't so much a restaurant as an Italian piazza, or gathering place, where political and intellectual discussion is as important as the cuisine. It provided the perfect atmosphere, along with excellent cuisine and hospitality for 120 guests.

PREFACE

When we started this series of talks on American Power in the fall of 2004, our intent was to break away from the large, impersonal lecture hall or hotel ballroom circuit. We wanted to return to the tradition of the intellectual "salon" where a smaller group of like-minded people could gather and enjoy an excellent meal followed by a stimulating exchange of ideas. And so the Grano Speakers Series began. The unique lectures reprinted here represent the first eight events held in Toronto from 2004 to 2006. They are unique because each speaker put away their notes and delivered their comments free of formalities and podium.

But the informality of the evening should not detract from the seriousness of the talks. The Grano series has attracted some of world's leading experts and thinkers on America's role in the world and the Middle East. The first series, from September 2004 to March 2005, featured four talks on the theme "America as an Imperial Power." Here our speakers were pundits William Kristol and Michael Ignatieff, political scientist Samuel P. Huntington (of *Clash of Civilizations* fame) and historian John Lukacs. The second series, from September 2005 to March 2006, featured another four speakers on the general topic of the Middle East: journalists Robert Kaplan and Christopher Hitchens, and academics Fouad Ajami and Bernard Lewis.

Do these talks hold up after so much has changed since they were given? The answer to that question is an unqualified yes. Each author reexamined their comments in early 2007 and revised them accordingly. As is to be expected when a number of different speakers address the same topic, not all follow the same thread or theme. But taken together, they provide an amazing glimpse into a particular moment in time, and offer a deeper understanding of the problems faced by the world's only superpower in a post-9/11 world.

—Rudyard Griffiths and Patrick Luciani
May 2007

PART I

THE AMERICAN EMPIRE

BIG CHANGES,
UNEXPECTED RESULTS

WILLIAM KRISTOL
SEPTEMBER 23, 2004

In this, the Grano Speakers Series inaugural lecture, William Kristol examines the impact of September 11, 2001, on American foreign policy in the Middle East and beyond. As both an insider in the Bush 41 administration and an editor of the influential Western Standard, *Kristol is a staunch defender of U.S. policy to overthrow the regime of Saddam Hussein. He is also closely connected to the neoconservative movement, which many associate with his father, Irving Kristol. For Kristol, 9/11 was a tragic interruption of a historical process—a process that was taking the world away from a Cold War paradigm to one based on globalization. September 11, 2001, heralded the arrival of a struggle against international terrorism. When change comes that quickly, Kristol argues, people are confused, and often end up choosing sides in unpredictable ways. As he delivered this talk, the Bush administration was facing mounting criticism over its handling of the Iraq invasion. The resulting discussions and debates came to dominate the lead up to the 2004 presidential election—a vote set to take place just five weeks after Kristol's talk.*

W e have lived through two very big changes in just fifteen years, and these changes have had deep ramifications. We all grew up in the Cold War era, which was the defining fact of American politics and world politics for forty years: from the late 1940s all the way to November 1989, when the Berlin Wall fell, and December 1991, when the Soviet Union disintegrated. We then adjusted to the 1990s, which was a remarkably different decade in terms of world and American politics. By definition, when you have a big change, all kinds of unexpected things happen that no one would have predicted.

Republicans have won the presidency for the last quarter century because they are tougher on national defense. The first President Bush thought he would win reelection in 1992 because he figured he had done what presidents were elected to do, which is to manage the national security interests of the country competently and responsibly. He did this. We won the Cold War with barely a shot fired, we kicked Saddam out of Kuwait and safeguarded the oil supplies upon which the whole world economy rests. But the Cold War had ended. The American people, as a consequence, didn't put as high a premium on national security experience or success. Bill Clinton, to his credit, saw this, ran on the economy and healthcare, and handily beat President Bush in the 1992 election.

The pattern in the last half of the Cold War was Republican president, Democratic Congress. Voters preferred the Democrats on domestic policy. They preferred the Republicans on foreign policy. They voted in a Democratic president and a Democratic Congress and after two years decided, "No, let's have a Republican Congress to check the Democratic president." And so, in 1996 there was a reversal of the Cold War pattern. Throughout the 1990s the U.S. was an evenly divided country: a Democratic president with an obviously Republican Congress. This culminated in the 2000 election, a totally evenly divided election at every level of government. Gore and Bush tied. The Senate tied. The House was virtually tied. Even at the state legislative level, the results were split. The impression was that America was an evenly divided country squabbling over domestic issues.

Foreign policy was barely an issue in the 2000 campaign. Jim Lehrer, the anchor of *The NewsHour* on PBS in the U.S., was the moderator for all three debates in 2000. Being a responsible guy, a serious guy, he knew that foreign policy was important. He insisted that half of one of the three debates between Vice President Gore and Governor Bush be on foreign policy. In 1996 there had been two debates between Clinton and Dole. The second was a town hall–type forum in San Diego where there were fifteen questions, fourteen of which were on domestic policy. One was on the trade deficit with Japan.

The mood of the 1990s was peace and prosperity. There were some problems in southeastern Europe, terrible things in Africa, but basically the world was a rosy place. In this context, the forty-five minutes of the Bush/Gore foreign policy debate in 2000 are quite striking. There was a lot of discussion of globalization and trade, some discussion of Milosevic and the Balkans, which was a fresh issue, and almost nothing about Iraq. There was bipartisan agreement that the United States could just contain Saddam. There was almost no discussion of weapons proliferation or Pakistan's testing of nuclear weapons. There was no mention of terrorism. No mention of Al Qaeda. No mention of Afghanistan. No mention of Osama bin Laden. The debate was quite even. Bush held his own, which was considered a victory since he was less experienced in foreign policy than Gore, and the campaign went right back to discussing Medicare and social security and the "lock box"—the catchphrase of the 2000 election campaign.[1]

The day after that debate, the USS *Cole* was attacked in Yemen at sea. Seventeen Americans were killed and about ninety people were wounded. Folks were shocked, obviously. It was the headline for two or three days. There was a little bit of sniping back and forth between Gore and Clinton, on the one hand, and Bush and the Republicans and Congress on the other, about who had let our guard down against terrorism. Then it faded right away. The *Weekly Standard* put a picture of the USS *Cole* at sea on its cover. It was kind of listing with this huge hole in its hull. It was a pretty famous picture at the time with a cover story by Reuel Marc Gerecht, who is a Middle East expert. The story was called "The U.S. at War" and tried

[1] Gore's promise not to allocate Social Security reserves to other areas of the budget.

to make the point that the U.S. needed to the see the attacks as a war, not just as individual, little terrorist problems that could be dealt with on an ad hoc basis or by law enforcement actions. Even the *Weekly Standard*, which was hawkish throughout the 1990s and denounced everyone's lack of interest in foreign policy, turned back to talking about domestic issues of the day within a week or two. It was just not an issue.

The 1990s was a good decade in many ways but it was a holiday from history in others, and certain problems were allowed to build up and to fester. One big difference between the U.S. and Europe now (and Canada is somewhere in between on this) is that Europe thinks 9/11 was a very unfortunate and tragic interruption in a historical process, which began with the end of the Cold War and could continue if only Bush weren't so irrational and headstrong and militaristic. Bush and most Americans, including many Democrats, think more than the 1990s ended on 9/11. That's a pretty startling fact. That means in just twelve to fifteen years we've gone through the destruction of one paradigm that everyone was comfortable with—the Cold War—and then we got used to another one: globalization. We debated all those issues and now we're in a third historical moment or era. I think when that kind of thing happens, especially in such quick succession, people are confused. People choose sides in different ways than one might expect. That has certainly been the case in America. The political dynamic has been reshuffled by 9/11. Governments sometimes react in somewhat chaotic and uncertain ways. Especially when they're surprised. It's really amazing.

Bush ran to be a domestic policy president. He didn't run on any foreign policy platform to speak of. If anything, during his debate with Gore he said that he hoped to have a more humble America. He was critical of Clinton and Gore for intervening too much overseas, but luckily Clinton and Gore were right on that one. There is an analogy with the early years of the Cold War. Truman expected to succeed Roosevelt and do the job of finishing the Second World War, bringing the troops home and getting back to normalcy. The G.I. Bill was passed so the soldiers could get educated, buy houses and get jobs while Truman could work on finishing the New Deal agenda. If you had predicted in 1945 or 1946 that we would remember Truman as a foreign policy president—as the architect of a doctrine that governed American foreign policy and the West's foreign policy for the next four decades—no one would have believed it. It was too fantastic a thought. No one predicted that America, a country that had never before deployed troops in Europe, would do so for forty years; that it would end up with permanent alliances in Europe and Asia, fight a ground war in Korea, institute the Marshall Plan and engage in Greece, Turkey and Berlin. It was all inconceivable. That's what happens when you have a real big sudden change. 9/11 may not quite be the Cold War, but it's a similar circumstance.

Bush, like Truman, has risen to the challenge of dramatic foreign policy developments in many ways. 9/11 was an unexpected challenge and one for which he was not particularly prepared, just as Truman wasn't particularly prepared in 1945. When he took over as president, Truman hadn't been briefed about the existence of the Manhattan Project or the atomic bomb. He had no knowledge about communism or European reconstruction or Korea. Those circumstances created difficult decisions, lots of bungling and lots of mistakes. Governments tend to be disorganized and conflicted. Truman's administration witnessed bitter, bitter fights between the executive office and the Defense and State Departments. Truman's Secretary of the Treasury, Henry Morgenthal, one of the most distinguished men in the U.S. government, seriously pushed a plan in 1945 and 1946 to deindustrialize Germany and turn it into a pastoral country. Politically, he reasoned, the U.S. couldn't afford to have a reindustrialized Germany. Truman's Secretary of State, George Marshall, the most respected man in the U.S. government, did not want Truman to recognize the State of Israel in 1947. Truman overruled him.

The Defense Department went through four defense secretaries in six years. Colin Powell, Secretary of State in the Bush administration from 2000 to 2004, is a huge admirer of George Marshall and there are great similarities. Marshall was a general who became Secretary of State and a great statesman, and I think Powell has always hoped to model himself after the general. The thought that Truman went through so many secretaries of defense must cheer him. But it was total chaos in 1945 and the Americans made some very bad mistakes.

The Korean War arguably happened because Dean Acheson, who was a great Secretary of State, foolishly defined the U.S. defense perimeter in a speech so as not to include Korea. This encouraged North Korea to invade the south with a huge cost to American and Canadian soldiers' lives, to say nothing of the Korean sacrifice. The post-9/11 environment is similar. Bush has made plenty of mistakes, especially after winning the war in Iraq. He failed to stop the looting, to provide security and to have enough troops to stabilize the situation early on. Once the insurgency began, it got harder to deal with and now, in the autumn of 2004, there is a very tough insurgency in the Sunni triangle. It's nasty and people are getting killed. Lots of Americans are dying; so are lots and lots of Iraqis. Iraqi terrorists kill a lot more Iraqis than they do Americans.

While there have been plenty of mistakes in Iraq, Bush deserves a pass on the grounds that it's extremely hard to manage situations you don't plan for and that your military didn't plan for. It is impossible to adjust quickly enough, although America should probably have adjusted better in some respects. American military, intelligence and diplomatic capabilities should all have been built up more quickly after 9/11. Trying to run a very aggressive Bush foreign policy with a 1990s-size military, a 1990s-size diplomatic establishment and a 1990s-size intelligence community is not adequate for the post-9/11 world. It seems unlikely these levels will change anytime soon. Even if Democrat John Kerry wins the 2004 election, there won't be any significant change on this front. Kerry is not going to become president and say, "Back to the status quo from today. Weapons of mass destruction? We'll just have to live with it if a couple more countries get nukes. Maybe we can negotiate an agreement with Korea or Iran.

That worked so well in the 1990s." That's not going to happen. Terrorism is going to be front and center of the foreign
policy agenda, no matter who the president is. Terrorism will
be the centerpiece of U.S. relations with countries ranging
from Saudi Arabia to Pakistan to the Palestinian Authority,
and that's not going to change if Kerry is president.

In the 1990s, the problem was not that America was too
imperial, to reference the title of this lecture series. The problem was not that we were too strong, that we intervened too
much or too soon or too rashly. The problem with the 1990s,
in retrospect, is that the U.S. was too timid and too slow, particularly in the Balkans and Rwanda. The United States was
certainly careless about terrorism and it ignored Afghanistan.
America was focusing only on its vital national interests and
worrying about trade with major commercial countries. It let
all kinds of things slide. It ignored the proliferation of
weapons of mass destruction by comforting itself with the
thought that the issues were being dealt with through multilateral and multinational processes that we hoped would
work. The truth is Abdul Qadeer Khan was having a merry
old time in Pakistan selling nuclear materials to Libya, Iran,
North Korea, China and Russia and trying to sell them to others. Iraq was involved in that, too.

It's to President Bush's credit, one of his unacknowledged
achievements, that he has actually shown leadership in bust-
ing up that nexus of proliferation. There is still a terrible
problem with North Korea and Iran, but I think it is incredible to look back at the 1990s, when all this stuff was
happening, and see that America was busy discussing a chem-

ical weapons treaty that would have been very nice for all the countries that had no intention of making or using chemical weapons anyway. They would cheerfully have signed it and patted each other on the back about how civilized they were, and meanwhile the proliferation of nuclear weapons would have continued. Many of the experts were earnestly assuring us not to worry: Sunni countries would never deal with Shiite countries and religious Islamic countries would never deal with secular countries. It turns out the Sunni Pakistanis were perfectly happy to sell stuff to the Shiite in Iran, and they were both perfectly happy to deal with secular Libya. Bush's instinct to go after the entire nexus of weapons of mass destruction proliferation, and states that sponsor terrorism, not just Al Qaeda or the Taliban, is accurate. Fundamentally, America has to be serious about changing the Middle East or, at least, changing the Arab world. You can't go into the twenty-first century with a huge chunk of the world being a home to increased extremism, terrorism, weapons of mass destruction development, anti-Americanism and anti-Western sentiments. This nexus had to be broken. How you do that and how you try to help construct modern pluralistic liberal democracies is a huge challenge.

Attempts to change the Middle East are often derided as Wilsonian or American messianism or American simple-mindedness, à la Jeffersonian democracy. However, most people realize that it is impossible to achieve Jeffersonian democracy in the Middle East immediately. There was no overnight Jeffersonian democracy in the United States. Canada, too, has had ethnic conflicts that, in living memory,

23

came close to threatening the integrity of the nation. The notion that we in the West have solved all these problems and that it's ridiculous to expect other countries to make any progress is preposterous. Bush is right to think that we can't return to the status quo. It turned out to be much more dangerous than we expected. The deals with the dictators were fueling resentment of the West. They were good recruiting tools for Osama bin Laden. Letting the Saudis export Wahhabi Islam was an unbelievable disaster and a sort of collective oversight by everyone in the West over the last twenty years. These things aren't easy to stop when dealing with a country like Pakistan or Saudi Arabia. Pressuring them toward reforms while not totally destabilizing them in the short term is a very dicey proposition. Nothing is going to fundamentally change in terms of the U.S. agenda, whether it's Bush or Kerry in the White House.

There was no such thing as an American empire in the 1990s, unless one uses that word in a very attenuated sense. Rather, one should think of American leadership in the world. The Canadian Prime Minister, Paul Martin, gave a talk at the UN and called for that organization to do all kinds of things. Most Americans would be thrilled if the UN did more, but we went through the 1990s, the Balkans and Rwanda. We went through the rise of terrorism and through Saddam, and the UN didn't do much to save lives in any of those situations. America often didn't, either.

Here is a practical question: Do people really think we can depend on the United Nations? Consider Sudan: A coalition of the willing could go in and force the government in

24

Khartoum to allow us to stop the attacks in Darfur or remove the regime there. We've waited on the UN for this. Sudan is exactly the kind of thing the UN should do. Iran is too big and too hard. Iraq is too complicated, but if ever there was a UN type of mission, Sudan is it. It is an unambiguous case of slaughter and ethnic cleansing. Except all the UN has done, as of the summer of 2004, is pass a toothless resolution saying essentially, "We'll consider sanctions down the road if Khartoum doesn't stop." The UN should be doing more but it's not going to happen in the very near future and, if no one does anything, the slaughter will continue. Without U.S. leadership, it's very hard for nations to get together to do anything.

Today, there is a much greater appetite for liberal interventionism, if not necessarily neoconservative interventionism, than there was in the 1990s. There was certainly a lot of talk about interventionism in the 1990s. In the debate between Gore and Bush in October 2000 they agreed that it was right not to have intervened in Rwanda, which is actually sort of shocking. Six years after 800,000 people are killed, the richest country in the world and the most powerful country in the world can't trouble itself to ask, "What would it have taken to act?" Five or ten thousand troops might not have saved all of the lives but they could have saved a lot. This inaction might not necessarily be repeated today and Sudan will be an interesting test.

Whoever becomes the next American president will have to intervene in Sudan. America can't sit by and let there be a second African genocide in ten years. There will be some liberal interventions. There will be more, tougher neoconservative interventions. This is the world we live in. There will be coalitions of the willing. Hopefully, alliance structures can be strengthened, particularly through enlargement of the North Atlantic Treaty Organization (NATO). One problem is that, post-9/11, the gulf between the U.S. and parts of Europe is wide both sociologically and culturally. There have always been differences but they were covered over by the Cold War. They were growing quietly in the 1990s and burst into full view after 9/11, especially in the debate over Iraq. Hopefully, the differences can be reconciled but they won't disappear entirely. America and Europe have different histories and different characters, and that fact of life has to be dealt with. We're not going to go back to the Cold War years and we're not going to go back to the '90s. The world will change as much in the next five years as it has in the last three. 9/11 has opened up all kinds of unanticipated consequences including, for example, a gulf between the U.S. and Europe. The future will hold more of these kinds of consequences. Things will look different to those who grew up in a certain era and are used to thinking of the world with the U.S., Europe, Canada and NATO as central. The U.S.-Indian relationship? It may end up being as important as the U.S.-German or U.S.-French ones from a strategic point of view. And that's not a bad thing. If one billion Indians come into relative prosperity in a democracy with a close alliance to Western countries, that would be a great accomplishment. It will, however, be different for us than what we're used to.

9/11 remains a very big deal in the U.S. and that is clear from the 2004 election, which is entirely a foreign policy election. The story of this election is Howard Dean's rise in 2003. It is unprecedented. No one has ever come from being a tiny governor of a pipsqueak state with no money, no name identification, to half a percent in the polls. He was a front-runner by the end of the year. Why? Not because of his domestic agenda. Not because of what he had to say about health care or any other social policy. It was because of the war. He opposed the war and a lot of Democrats thought Bush was wrong to take the U.S. into Iraq. A lot of voters thought it was a terrible mistake that the Democrats in Washington didn't have the guts to oppose Bush. Why did Dean fall at the end of 2003? Only because he seemed too extreme and because he seemed unelectable.

Kerry and Edwards voted against the $87 billion to support the troops and reconstruction in Iraq, which is really ridiculous. How can you vote *for* the war and *against* the money to pay for it? There were only four senators who voted for the war and against the $80-plus billion. Two of them were Kerry and Edwards. It was entirely a political vote, which is understandable. They were running for president. But it was a vote that allowed them to signal to the Dean supporters, "We're now antiwar. Yes, we voted for the war, but now we're kind of going in an antiwar direction." Kerry had the Vietnam service. People thought that would make him more electable vis-à-vis Bush, so Kerry beat Dean.

That's the story of the Democratic primary: entirely foreign-policy driven just as the general election has been entirely foreign-policy driven. Kerry feels that he has to establish himself as a post-9/11 commander in chief. He can't just be a traditional Democrat, worrying about health care and education. But his way of accomplishing this, which was slightly odd, was to emphasize that he served in Vietnam. He had this whole show at the Democratic convention where he and his band of brothers went over his Vietnam service record a million times. He didn't quite think it through, though. There are two issues with Kerry's approach: first, a lot of people, as much as they may have admired his service in Vietnam, resented what he did when he came back and spoke against the war and, to some degree, against the soldiers who were still fighting there. The issue rose up from the dead, so to speak, along with his service in Vietnam. Secondly, people don't care what you did thirty years ago. They want to know what you're going to do to lead the country post-9/11. So the Republicans were able to counterattack.

Bush had a very successful convention. People like John McCain and Rudy Giuliani are not Bush Republicans and therefore have more credibility when they speak on his behalf because their support is not automatic. At the convention, they stood up and said in pretty strong speeches that, "This man, whatever our differences with him [that part was implied], has been a strong leader, a strong commander in chief." The convention moved the electorate and the swing voters by several percentage points. Bush is now ahead and Kerry's perfectly intelligent gambit is to say, "Look, Bush got us into Iraq. It's a horrible mess. It's Vietnam. We're losing. It's getting worse and I'll get you out one way or another. At the very least, I will sort of change course and magically get the Europeans to come in." The idea that after telling voters for the next two months what a horrible, horrible mess Iraq is that the Europeans are going to cheerfully come in is a little fanciful, but nonetheless, it's what you do if you're the opposing candidate. Kerry's not going to say we're going to get out. He's not going to say we're going to escalate. He's just saying it's time for a change, just as Dwight D. Eisenhower said in 1952 running against Stevenson after Korea. Nixon said it in 1968 against Hubert Humphrey, Johnson's vice-president. It worked for those two so it's not a foolish move. However, it's a little risky because it puts you on the side of seeming to root for defeat or predicting bad news when the U.S. has 150,000 troops stationed overseas. People don't really want to hear about how bad things are getting. Kerry will have a chance at the presidency if things seem to get visibly worse and increasingly out of control in Iraq.

The debates remain very important. People shouldn't assume anything. I'm for Bush and I'm happy with the current state of play where Bush is up by about five points over Kerry. Still, Gore was up by about five at this time in 2000 and everyone thought Gore was a better debater than Bush. If you read the transcripts, Gore *was* actually better than Bush in a technical sense but he came off in such a bad way that Bush ended up benefiting from the debates and then went ahead in the polls. Gore caught up to him at the end and then they had an even election. That could happen this time or it might not. Or Bush could continue to open up an even bigger lead. I don't know. But in any case, it is a post-9/11 election. That's the most important thing about it.

The 2008 election is also going to be a post-9/11 election just as 1948 and 1952 were Cold War elections. Nine-eleven isn't going away in the near future. The Bushes are very family oriented and they have long memories. Either you're with them or you're against them. Successful politicians are often that way. I am not a Bush loyalist or apologist, but I will say this about Bush. The day before the 2000 vote, Bush was campaigning on education policy and concluded a luncheon speech by saying that it was very important that every American parent, each American mother and father, ask himself or herself the following question: "Is our children learning?" Which is a good question. I ask my wife, Susan, that quite often. So everyone laughed and Bush said, "You know, I don't always speak English so well but people know what I mean." And then Bush, in a series of speeches over the next few hours all across the country, repeated the story and turned it into a joke on himself and would say he was actually learning and everyone would laugh. And finally, near the end of the day, Bush told the story again and everyone laughed and Bush paused and sort of reflected for a minute and said, "You know, I've found it's a great advantage in politics to have one's opponents misunderestimate you." If you asked me to predict what will happen in the election in five weeks, and more broadly in terms of the Bush presidency, I would say that it may be the case that Bush's opponents both at home and abroad have pretty consistently misunderestimated him.

———

Q: If there is the return of history, 9/11 may well be a defining characteristic of a new world order, I don't know. The return is to the medieval. It's not the Cold War. The Cold War was really very convenient because Marx was a child of the Enlightenment, the same as Adam Smith.

Now we're dealing with religious fundamentalists and the only thing that would be similar would be the Crusades. So we're dealing with something that we can't even comprehend. Let's use Harry Truman and the Marshall Plan and the creation of a postwar world as an example. In Japan, they were dealing with the embedded institutional structure of quite an advanced country. What is the embedded institutional structure of fundamentalist Islam? What does the word democracy mean? This is pre-pre-Enlightenment.

A: I don't agree. Obviously, the Cold War is an analogy. We're in a new moment and we can't go back to the Cold War. First of all, there were embedded institutional structures in Germany and Japan. There certainly weren't deeply embedded *democratic* structures there. The problem of Islam or the problem of Islam in the Arab world, in particular, is a very deep and challenging one, but it has to be dealt with, and it can't be dealt with by just saying the word democracy. But it also can't be dealt with just by saying it's medieval so we can't do anything about it. It's not medieval, incidentally. This kind of Islam is a weird combination, called Islamo-

31

Fascism by people like Christopher Hitchens and Paul Berman. There's a lot of truth to that term. Wahhabi Islam is not traditional Islam. Wahhabi Islam is modern and was not powerful thirty years ago. It was confined pretty much to Saudi Arabia.

Unfortunately, we all allowed the Saudis to export it all around the Islamic world and it is now destabilizing places that had a rather relaxed, modernizing and friendly Islam. Pakistan, Indonesia and Malaysia were not full of crazed, religious fundamentalists who were blowing themselves up. They had all kinds of problems that Third World countries have, but they did not have this particular problem.

Wahhabi Islam has risen up more recently than we sometimes think and I think it could be beaten back. Then the question is how to do it. It could be done just by pure force, by making it too expensive to indulge in, by putting out of business the people who recruit and pay for it, and the states that harbor it especially.

If you had said Afghanistan was going to be a center for the Taliban thirty years ago, it would have been thought ridiculous. Afghanistan had no tradition of that. Afghanistan was a weird tribal kind of place, but it wasn't a Taliban-type place. They took over because they had the power to do so and because no one went in to kick them out. I'm pretty optimistic that Afghanistan actually will end up being a perfectly decent, peaceful place with a lot of tribes modernizing gradually and not posing a threat to anyone. I think other parts of the Middle East could develop this way too: Jordan, Tunisia, Morocco. These are real countries. They're moving, more or less, in a decent direction. Egypt has a real liberal, modernizing tradition, though it's complicated there, too.

You can't automatically apply the paradigm of the Cold War. This is a new challenge and it requires new thinking but it does have to be dealt with. We can't just pretend to ignore that whole part of the world and hope that those guys don't develop weapons that could kill huge numbers of Americans or Canadians or anyone else. Bush's instinct is right. Sometimes his rhetoric may sound a little grandiose about freedom and democracy, but he's basically right. The Middle East should be assisted in making a transition that will be difficult, but I don't think we have much choice. Truman and the Cold War are not a perfect analogy by any means, but I do think this is a really new challenge that people need to do some fresh thinking about.

Q: The United States is incurring incredible, incredible deficits in order to go to war in Iraq. You have a president who has said, "Yes, we are going to have a major incursion geopolitically. We are going to war. We are going to Iraq and yet, you will not have to pay for it," and these massive deficits have incurred, something that conservatives have adamantly objected to. There has to be a great divide in the conservative wing in the United States.

A: There are some who are more concerned about it than others. The deficit is about 3.6 percent of the current GDP, which is less than the 5.5 percent it reached under Reagan, so it's affordable and I would actually defend Bush's tax cuts, though maybe not every last detail. But generally, the stimulative effect of those tax cuts has led the U.S. to have the fastest economic growth in the Western world.

As an aside, Canada has actually been a great beneficiary of this engine of growth. The U.S. is going to have to curb spending on some domestic programs, which no one wants to do. I don't think we're going to be able to curb military or diplomatic or intelligence spending and I myself would, in fact, be for increasing it. Right now, even with the huge supplemental, even with Iraq, we are spending probably about 4.2, 4.3 percent of GDP on defense. Let's throw in intelligence and diplomacy and let's say we're spending a nickel of every dollar on foreign policy, which is about right. It's way under the Cold War numbers, which averaged about 6.5 percent. It's totally affordable. We may have to take a tax increase to pay for it at some point, but I wouldn't have raised taxes in the last two or three years. I think it was wise in a recession to be stimulative in a fiscal policy.

If we have to raise taxes a little bit, we'll raise taxes a little bit. I'm not really alarmed. Other conservatives are more hawkish on the deficit than I am, but I think the money we're spending abroad is certainly worth spending. If anything, we're not spending enough on military intelligence. I would kill a lot of the domestic programs but there's not much public support for that. If the deficit persists, the political system will react as it did in the 1990s. But right now, Alan Greenspan [Chairman of the Federal Reserve] raised the interest rates to 1.75 percent. It's hard to tell people that we're paying a big price for this deficit and, honestly, this is a democracy, so when we're paying a price, we'll react.

Q: In the Cold War, the United States led the free world. At the time, I think it was the German statesman Willy Brandt who said, "The one thing we worry about here in Germany in terms of you protecting our interests and protecting us from the threat of the Soviet power is whether the U.S. will be in it for the long haul." It's a real question that those who rely implicitly or explicitly on American power and American determination always have to ask. What is the capacity of the American people to sustain these kinds of open-ended commitments? There's no question that with the Middle East remediation project, Bush has undertaken a huge open-ended commitment, not unlike the Cold War. It's a very, very large-scale commitment in historical terms. In a world where the United States is doing this more or less alone, with extremely limited support from its allies and where the American public rather enjoyed those 1990s (which were arguably a holiday from history), how do you feel about the sustainability of American commitment in Iraq where a greater level of commitment is required in a later age, much more removed from the challenges of the 1930s, 1940s and 1950s, which really called Americans to greatness?

A: I think your last sentence really gives away a deep difference in perspective. It's not a later age for us. It's three years after 9/11. As long as the commitment is seen as preventing further and bigger 9/11s, I think it's going to be an easy thing to convince a democracy that it should spend huge amounts of money 10,000 miles away for apparently ungrateful people who, in any case, are odd from our point of view in terms of religion and culture. It's not that we're closer to 9/11 than the Cold War years were to any Soviet takeover of Eastern Europe or the beginning of the Second World War. The idea of a later age has a certain kind of view of history as moving away from the use of force and that this is the shape of the world we're in, and I don't think Americans share that sense of the world. Obviously, many Europeans do.

The worry about America's commitment, and that of its public, is legitimate. It was a worry throughout the Cold War. If you had said in 1946 or 1947, "You know what? The American people are going to support 300,000 troops in Europe as well as 50,000 in Japan and 35,000 more in Korea. Then the U.S. is going to fight a war in Korea and then one in Vietnam," it would have been incredible. No one would have thought, given U.S. history, that we could do it, but we did do it. That doesn't mean there weren't all kinds of problems in doing it. We did have more allies, though, in truth. The allies in the European case were just sitting there so it wasn't very hard for them to be allies. Most of the heavy lifting, I think it's fair to say, was done by the U.S. in terms of serious defense expenditures and serious troop numbers based overseas. It's a striking fact that for all the talk or the implication that the U.S. public is always itching to come home, there was support even in the 1990s for substantial defense expenditure and for involvement in the Balkans in December 1995. Admittedly, no Americans were killed in Bosnia. It was a successful intervention that helped Clinton get reelected.

Americans were happy to see America actually playing a role in stopping ethnic cleansing and showing leadership in the world. Clinton was hurt in '93 and '94 when we pulled out of Somalia and looked kind of helpless. I don't think one should underestimate the extent to which Americans, with good leadership, are willing to assume international burdens if they think (a) it's the right thing to do, if it's helping people; and (b) that it's in our interest. We are defending ourselves. I think Bush has done a good job of saying, "Look, this is kind of an abstract performance in the Middle East but we know what happens when we don't do this. We know what happens to us if we have an unreformed Middle East and that's just not acceptable. We would prefer to have more people with us, but we do what we have to do."

In November 2003, I was in Europe when Bush announced that we were going to try to have a transition to Iraqi control with an interim Iraqi government on July 1, 2004. I was a little worried that this was just a fancy exit strategy. Actually, Bob Kagan and I went to see Condoleezza Rice. She assured us, "No, it really isn't. It's actually a way that will make it easier for us to fight and win the war." This may be true and I hope it is. Based on Iyad Allawi's performance so far, it could well be true.

In Europe, all the top government officials and intellectuals were saying, "Well, of course. Bush is getting out. This is an exit strategy," and I would earnestly say, "No, it really isn't. You know, we're not really going to cut and run. Obviously, any president would love to be able to reduce troop levels if it's doable. If it's not, he'll keep them there. He might even increase them." I don't think people thought I was crazy; I think they thought I was lying to them. I can't tell you how many times I heard them say, "Karl Rove will not allow George Bush to go to reelection with 120,000 [as it was then] U.S. troops in Iraq, taking casualties from roadside bombs and suicide bombers every day." Note that since then Bush has increased U.S. forces in Iraq. I myself would have increased them a little more, but he has increased them to 150,000. We're taking bad casualties and he's running for reelection and, actually, he's a little bit ahead.

If Bush loses, then I think one fair question to Kerry will be, does he take his victory as a lesson that the public isn't willing to support the intervention in Iraq or does he just take it as a lesson that Bush did it badly? Over the last year Bush has increased troop strength in a war that has not gone well, where there is by no means overwhelming support for the war in the U.S. and where we're taking casualties. Still, Bush is running for reelection on Iraq and not shrinking from it at all.

I think that's to his credit, personally. But also I think it does say something about the American public's considerable tolerance for this if they think it's important and essential and if they think it's winnable. I mean, obviously if it's just hopeless then no one supports spending more money and giving up more lives, but if there's a plausibly decent and improving outcome, I think it has a surprising amount of support.

Q: The Cold War ended and we moved into a period where people got to be more and more selfish. We even had Al Franken's "Me Decade." What we're really interested in is, what does it mean for Canada? What does this new age mean about the way you think about allies, and what does it mean about allies like us who are part of the civilized humanity, but would really instinctively prefer it if occasionally we had the right to cheese you off without affecting our income stream?

A: I think the Bush administration has, in some respects, done a bad job of alliance management and maintenance. I don't think they're just a bunch of unilateral, headstrong folks who don't care. They do care. They just have not been very competent when it comes to normal diplomacy. I don't include in this the failure to get France and Germany on board with the Iraq war. They weren't going to join anyway and I think they had every right not to join. It's a decision sovereign governments get to make. I think to the degree that France went around trying to prevent us from getting others to join, we have a bit of an issue with them but it's not as if their actions over Iraq totally destroyed U.S.-France relations. It's not as if there aren't a million different ways in which we continue to work together.

I'm not sure what happens to alliances at a time like this. We are in a very early moment. Do we continue a kind of Cold War model of permanent alliances, like NATO? I hope so. I think that's a healthy thing. Is it supplemented by coalitions of the willing? Of course, we forget how much of that there was in the Cold War years. Korea, Vietnam, the Gulf War. These were all, in a sense, coalitions of the willing. I think there will be more of that.

Any U.S. administration will be particularly grateful and think well of allies who share American values and principles. We'll think better of allies that put themselves on the line for us, and work with us. I don't honestly think right now there's any great resentment against Canada in the United States. There's probably not as much of a sense as there was in the 1980s that we should bend over backwards to you. If there's some mad cow roaming around who's going to get into the U.S., there's probably less political will to overrule that on the grounds that it's really important to reward Canada for geopolitical or strategic reasons.

But I don't think people are upset. Frankly, it's not a big issue in the sense that the U.S. has a gradation of relationships depending on particular issues. To the degree that there were hopes in the 1980s and 1990s of a grand, strategic bargain between the U.S. and Canada, what we have now is somewhat different. I don't know that the U.S. and Canada are fundamentally different, but we do have somewhat different takes on the world we live in, the use of force, the role of the UN and so on.

When you see Bush's speech to the UN and Prime Minister Paul Martin's speech to the UN, you see that Canada and the U.S. are not entirely on the same wavelength. We can live with that. We won't be as close as we were in the 1980s, but there's not going to be bitter retribution either. Canada and the U.S. will just be somewhat different countries living safely, in a neighborly way, next to each other. I think the administration, whoever it is, would approach Canadian-American issues on an ad hoc basis.

The great comedy about John Kerry is that he's a great multilateralist. He speaks fluent French. He went to school in Switzerland. It's all so wonderful. His great criticism of Bush is that we've alienated all kinds of countries, which Americans have a sort of ambivalent view about. His solution in Iraq, which I think is sort of fanciful, is to have all these European troops come in. Kerry is going to have a tough time if he gets elected. I don't think he can cut and run in Iraq and he's going to go to France and be very charming and speak French to them and say, "I got elected. I beat Bush. That's what you guys wanted. So now help out. We'd like ten thousand French troops in Baghdad and we've got an assault on Fallujah planned. We'd really like to have your special forces in that."

Of course, Chirac will look at him like he's crazy. There will be a bigger crisis in U.S.-European relations if Kerry is elected than if Bush is, because the expectations are so out of control: "He doesn't care about us and Kerry is going to take us back to the 'good old days,'" which weren't necessarily the good old days, needless to say. The phrase "hyperpuissance" was invented when Clinton was president, not Bush. Nonetheless, there's such a myth now about the pre-Bush age that if Kerry wins there will be a genuine crisis in U.S.-European relations.

Q: I don't think the U.S. can cut and run from Iraq but I'm haunted by the Vietnam parallel. Within three years of the departure of the last American from Vietnam, just about every American foreign policy objective in southeast Asia was more or less achieved. Instead of the domino effect, we had Vietnam invading Cambodia. We had China invading Vietnam. Is there perhaps a lesson in what could never have been predicted, that the area left alone would return to its traditional devices?

A: Two or three million dead was a pretty high price to pay in Vietnam and Cambodia. And I don't agree. Vietnam was a terrible defeat for us. The U.S. and the Western world had a terrible last half to the 1970s. Luckily the Soviet Union was weaker than we thought. I don't believe the end of the Cold War was as inevitable as people think. Historical fact will show a few world leaders who came to power in very unexpected and very surprising ways. Reagan won, proceeded with a huge defense buildup, put pressure on the Soviet Union and we ended up doing okay. I personally think that's what could happen in this case. We'll have the short-term disaster, but over the longer term we won't allow major Middle East nations to be taken over by terrorists.

I think (a) we won't cut and run; and (b) if it were to happen, it would have very bad short-term consequences. The one difference is that Vietnam was one front in the Cold War. It was not the major front, which was Europe. Vietnam was a damaging defeat, but we were able to rally and hold the other fronts and then come back in other ways. Iraq is the central front on the war against terror. Right now, we are fighting the terrorists there. No one can deny that. And if Zarqawi wins and we are chased out, I think the implications of that are really terrible. It is analogous to losing Greece and Turkey or Berlin in 1947 or 1948. The U.S. can't actually afford to get out and that's why if Kerry wins he'll end up pursuing a rather similar policy to Bush.

Q: There have been some obvious parallels tonight between the Cold War and the post-9/11 war that we're in. Not without dissent, but Canada generally, over a long period of time, supported the U.S. side in the Cold War. This was made easier because it wasn't just the U.S. side. It was an alliance of Western nations. It was also made a lot easier because there was a constant appeal to universal principles—liberty, democracy, economic liberty, freedom.

It's not clear that those same principles shouldn't apply to the new war we're in. The difference is that the U.S. nomenclature is about this being for U.S. national interests. This makes it much more difficult to be a Canadian supporter of the side of liberalism or liberty in the post-9/11 war, particularly the Iraq War. Has the United States wrongly mischaracterized or mispositioned this struggle as a defense of U.S. interests rather than seeing 9/11 as an attack on universal principles? Has this mischaracterization actually made it more difficult for allies to come onside, particularly an ally like Canada that sees itself as a mirror of what happens in the U.S.?

A: The usual criticism of Bush's rhetoric is the opposite, that it's too universalistic, too general in its references to democracy and freedom. Whatever happened to good old-fashioned realpolitik and hard-headed containment of certain dictators? Why all this talk about spreading freedom around the world?

9/11 happened to be an attack on New York and Washington. It could have been on Montreal or Toronto, but it wasn't. The idea of a defense against 9/11 and not allowing another 9/11 to happen is very particular to the U.S. The fact that we led the coalition in the first Gulf War against Saddam had a certain U.S.-centric focus as well. To sell this in the U.S., any American president is going to emphasize that American interests and principles are at stake. I think Bush has tried to cast this in sort of a universalistic light. Frankly, we could protect ourselves better than a lot of other nations if the Middle East falls apart and people get weapons of mass destruction and terrorist groups become more powerful. We are big and strong and we have this big ocean between us and them, and we probably could do a kind of Fortress America a lot more successfully than other people. The deeper question is: Do we share the same understanding of the universal principles? I don't think that America's rhetoric is nationalistic and Canada is universalistic. I think we have one universalistic view of freedom advancing in the world and the importance of being willing to sacrifice and use force for the sake of that and confronting terror wherever it exists.

You have to take sides—one side or the other, for or against the terrorists. That kind of Bush-type rhetoric stands in contrast to Kofi Annan–sort rhetoric, or EU rhetoric, which worries much more about international law, international consensus, respecting sovereign states and working things out through diplomacy and negotiation and the like.

Maybe what we have is two competing universalisms, an American one and a European one. Kagan called it Kant universalism versus Lockian universalism, which may be a little misleading. They're both universalist; they just have a different view of how the world works and what can succeed in a world where not everyone is liberal and not everyone is tolerant and not everyone is civilized and not everyone is law abiding.

I think a lot of it comes down to what you really think the world is like in the twenty-first century and whether Bush's sense of how to make the world safer is correct. Kofi Annan is a very nice man. He makes very nice speeches. But to use a Machiavellian term, the effectual truth of Kofi Annan is Srebrenica and it's Rwanda. It's doing nothing. Bush can make mistakes, too, God knows, but at least there's an attempt to mobilize the forces of the civilized world against these terrible threats.

CANADA AND THE
WANING OF U.S. PRIMACY

MICHAEL IGNATIEFF
NOVEMBER 18, 2004

Michael Ignatieff gave his lecture before he was approached by the Liberal Party of Canada to run for parliament, and before he made a run at the party leadership. Ignatieff, who was teaching at Harvard's John F. Kennedy School of Government at the time of his talk, argues that although the United States may once have been an empire, those days are gone. Although Ameri may indeed maintain a certain primacy in world affairs—a primacy based on military and economic might—even this form of power is being eroded by a perceived lack of legitimacy. In other words, there are limits to American power, and smaller countries such as Canada can exercise influence without threat of retaliation—if they are willing to shoulder some of the burden.

W hat *is* America? How are we to think of the power that it exerts in the world? Is it an empire? Although I myself have used the word "empire" to characterize American power, I'm unhappy with it. Empire means the colonial acquisition, management and administration of territory without the consent of its inhabitants. In the Philippines, in Haiti, in Cuba, America once did exercise imperial power in this strict sense. But no longer.

If you want to understand American power you've got to have a precise sense of what the United States actually does in the world. It's not an empire because it does not have colonies in any traditional meaning of the word, not even in Iraq. It doesn't have satrapies; that is, nominally independent states that are actually under its control. Empires have satrapies; they don't have allies. Canada, for example, would count as an ally, not as a satrap.

If we want to know what an empire actually is or was, we should think of the Soviet Union. Poland and Hungary, for example, understood what an empire was. The Soviets marched into their territory, tossed governments out and imprisoned and killed those who resisted. Think of Budapest in 1956 or Prague in 1968. That is what we're talking about when we speak of empire. Any other usage is just metaphor.

If empire does not capture what America does in the world, is hegemon a better option? That's the second option, but it also is an implausible description since it exaggerates America's actual power in the world. America cannot be described as a hegemon in East Asia, where China is the rising power. True, since the Korean War, America provides security guarantees to South Korea, Japan and Taiwan, and has guaranteed their independence against any hostile intentions by the Chinese. But a true hegemon would have been able to force China to ally with its own attempt to prevent North Korea from acquiring nuclear weapons. Hegemons get their way. America's power in East Asia is significant but not hegemonic.

Nor is it hegemonic in Europe. It may have been a hegemon right after the Second World War, when it helped Europe back on its feet with the Marshall Plan, rudely cutting British ambitions back to size while containing Soviet expansionism in Greece, Italy and Eastern Europe. Perhaps it remained a hegemon in Europe through the Berlin crisis of 1962. Thereafter, as the European community began to come together and the Germans under Willy Brandt began to reach out to the Soviet bloc, pursuing an Ostpolitik increasingly independent of the Americans, Europeans themselves began to challenge American hegemony in Europe. From de Gaulle onward every French president has set it as his major task to challenge American dominance in Europe. In the Franco-German alliance of the Cold War, both countries succeeded in consolidating European independence on the world stage. With the end of the Cold War and the withdrawal of both Soviet and American forces from Europe, the Europeans think of their Union as a power in its own right, and though the European project of further integration has stalled, American influence there has waned. Notice, for example, the rising importance of the euro as a global currency. It does not rival the dollar, but it will.

As for Africa, America is not a hegemon in Africa because nobody in Washington seems to believe that Africa matters. A truly global hegemon would be watching out for countries such as Zaire or Zimbabwe, as they tumble into chaos and drag down every country around them. Instead, Africa is part of the world that has dropped off the map as far as America is concerned. Indeed, China may already exercise more economic and political influence in Africa than the United States.

The United States is not a hegemon in the Middle East. It may once have been, in the period initiated by Franklin Roosevelt's famous meeting with Ibn Saud on his return from Yalta. First under Roosevelt and then under Truman, the United States anchored its authority in the Middle East on two pillars: Saudi oil and Israeli democracy. Right through until the Yom Kippur War of 1973, when Kissinger was able to determine exactly how far both Israel and Egypt could go, America was the decisive player. No more. The high-water mark of American influence may have been the Camp David accords negotiated by President Carter. Since then, the story has been one of ebbing influence over historical events. The American security guarantee to Israel is as strong as ever, but the rise of Shia militancy in Lebanon, the emergence of Hamas in Palestine, the ascendancy of Iran, the collapse of order in Iraq have all occurred despite America's best efforts. Not even the Israelis can be counted on to obey American orders. Israel's independence of action and the Saudi regime's increasingly autonomous proposals for the peace process contradict any image of an all-powerful America moving the pieces around on the chessboard of the Middle East.

The most we can say about the United States is that it exercises a kind of primacy in world affairs. This primacy is based, first of all, on military preponderance. The U.S. still spends more than all of its other military competitors combined. But overwhelming military preponderance does not produce hegemonic control. Nothing illustrates the pathos of American military preponderance better than Iraq, where the world's most powerful and skilled military is struggling to contain an ever-growing insurgency and a civil war. Not since Vietnam has American military power seemed so impotent in the face of determined enemies. America's rivals, China and Russia, must be watching with glee as the U.S. flounders ever deeper into the quagmire. Extrication from Iraq may conserve American military power, but extrication, as in Vietnam, will diminish its influence. Successful withdrawal is likely to leave the American political elite—and American voters—circumspect about the future interventions, whether nation-building or protecting populations at risk.

The second source of American primacy, of course, is economic power. Here too, however, the balance is changing. In 1945, the U.S. truly dominated the global economy, and this predominance persisted until the first oil shocks of the 1970s. American leadership in key sectors—software, services, biotech and other science-based technologies—endures, but if the twentieth century belonged to America, because of its huge internal market, its hard-working labor force and its ferocious capacity for innovation, it seems more likely that the twenty-first century will belong to India and China.

The third source of American primary in the twentieth century was cultural: the sheer attractiveness of the American model—the association between consumerism and freedom—and the allure of American popular culture. But again, the heyday of American cultural predominance may already lie in the past: from the amazing cultural flowering that was jazz in the 1920s to rhythm and blues and rock 'n' roll in the 1950s and 1960s. It was then that, for Eastern Europeans locked inside the gray-on-gray of Soviet rule, for Western Europeans rebuilding after the war, for Africans and Asians seeking freedom from colonial rule, that American music seemed to carry a message of freedom and pleasure. That period is now a memory. Indeed the period of uncontested American hegemony in culture was brief, and now the push back is all the other way. In cinema, television, fashion and music, we live in a world where the trends are set in London, Mumbai and Milan as much as in New York or Los Angeles.

The cultural allure of the United States went hand in hand with the power of its egalitarian social model and its progressive liberal politics. For liberal thinkers in Canada and Europe, Roosevelt, Truman and Kennedy were inspirations: first in the incorporation of organized labor, second in the positive vision of the role of government and third in the campaigns to strike down social injustice. Civil rights was never just an American movement: it inspired freedom-loving men and women everywhere. When the civil rights movement lost impetus in the 1960s, when the reaction that led to Reagan set in, liberals worldwide ceased to look to America for inspiration. Instead, conservatives in Britain, France and Germany looked to the Reagan revolution for their models. Yet America's capacity to inspire political movements elsewhere may now be waning.

So we can summarize the American position in the world as one of contested primacy, but not of hegemony or empire. It is not merely that America faces peer competitors, like Russia, China and, soon, India. In addition, American primacy is exercised as power but the power lacks the authority that comes with legitimacy, the consensual acceptance that its rule is justified or just. To a degree unprecedented since Vietnam, American power appears to the world simply as naked force.

The question is, where has the legitimacy gone? One source of legitimacy for American power after 1945 was the presence of the Soviet Union as an evil empire. Whatever else most liberal democrats thought about America, they knew that the Soviet regime was demonstrably worse. The mere existence of the Soviet system legitimized American power, and turned most of its exercises of power into legitimate authority. Standing up to the Soviet blockade of Berlin in 1948 was legitimate; denouncing the Soviet takeover of Hungary was legitimate; seeking to prevent Soviet expansion into the Horn of Africa in the 1970s and then into Afghanistan were all widely accepted as legitimate, at least by America's allies. From 1945 to 1989, whatever difficulties Canada had with our relations with the Americans, we knew that we were yoked with them in a battle with a Soviet regime we knew to be much worse. The disappearance of the Soviet threat after 1989 has had the effect of delegitimizing the sole power that remains. What the Soviet system could not achieve with its power, it has achieved, ironically enough, with its collapse.

It was inevitable that American primacy after the end of the Cold War would generate resistance. Europe sees its role in the world to serve as a counterpower to American primacy. The Russians under Putin see their task as rebuilding Russian glory after the years of forced humiliation under Yeltsin and Gorbachev. China likewise sees opportunities in the decaying legitimacy of American primacy.

Since the U.S. embassy siege of 1979, Iran has seen itself, likewise, as the leader of the Shia Islamic challenge to U.S. power in the Middle East. First Iran humiliated the U.S. during the hostage-taking, destroying Carter's presidency, then it sought to humiliate Reagan through the bombing of the Marine detachment in Beirut. By financing Hezbollah and Hamas, Iran now challenges Israel directly, and in developing nuclear power in defiance of the world, Iran has set itself up as the chief challenger to American primacy in the Middle East.

The passing of American primacy has been hastened by the country's own mistakes—chief of which is Iraq—but it might have happened anyway. No single country can hope to reproduce, indefinitely, the dominance that America enjoyed between 1945 and 1989. Economic developments alone, favoring the resurgence of Russia, China and India, would put a term to American predominance, and ideological factors, like the stubborn power of Shia Islam, would inevitably generate resentment and resistance toward American designs in the Middle East.

The passage of American primacy may be inevitable, and it may not even be dismaying, provided that the emerging balance of power is stable and peaceful. There is no reason to be nostalgic for American hegemony. It's not good to have too much power concentrated in anyone's hands in the world. Far better to have a global system, with multiple poles of power, each competing and checking the other. Provided of course, that these powers meet, establish minimum multi-lateral frameworks to prevent overt conflicts of interest; provided that they communicate clearly with each other; provided that they do not seek to upset the balance by unilateral acts of expansion or aggression.

Many questions follow from this analysis. What strategies, if any, exist for America to recover primacy? Should it even try? Or should it seek instead to manage the emergence of a multipolar and multilateral world?

There's a liberal agenda to recover legitimacy and it is to make America submit to a multilateral order. Here the project entails a kinder, gentler America that reenlists itself in the multilateral order, that endorses Kyoto and ICC [International Criminal Court], that reinvests in the UN, the WTO and other international institutions. Such a vision of America is attractive to liberals, but it makes a difficult trade-off. According to this trade-off, America sacrifices unilateral exercises of power, even a modicum of national sovereignty, for the gains in acceptance, approval and legitimacy that accrue by signing up to a multilateral order. This kind of bargain works where the interests at stake are marginal, for example, in Darfur, where America might be willing to allow multilateral actors to take a lead, even to constrain American ambitions in the region, for the sake of the reputational gains that would accrue to America if it were seen to be on the side of a durable peace in Sudan. It is less clear that the liberal recovery of legitimacy through multilateral engagement works as well where America's vital national interests are at stake. Yet even here, burden-sharing with allies seems especially attractive after Iraq. An America that feels overstretched and underappreciated may find reengagement in the UN and its agencies an attractive option. The question is whether the U.S. is willing to accept any substantial abridgment of its own freedom of action. Will it be willing, for example, to work with the International Criminal Court and accept that if it wants the Court to be effective, it will have to accept the Court's ultimate mandate over U.S. citizens? At the moment, this seems out of the question because it is unpopular and very hard to sell to the American public, used as it is to unchallenged primacy. Yet this trade-off—getting other nations to share its burdens, while accepting some diminution of its own freedom of action—seems essential if American power is to regain legitimacy.

Certainly the conservative solution to the problem of eroding American legitimacy has been a fiasco. The Bush-Cheney strategy was to legitimize unilateralism and hence American primacy through military success. The result has been Iraq.

Yet conservative failure does not ensure liberal success. Failure in Iraq does not guarantee the reemergence of a kinder, gentler and, above all, more prudent and multilateral America. America was ambivalent about multilateralism even in the days when it dominated the multilateral order. It is likely to be even more ambivalent now that its primacy is a thing of the past. It will be a difficult matter for Democrats to convince a sorely tried American electorate of the counterintuitive proposition that legitimacy is best enhanced by allowing Gulliver to be tied down by leading strings. For this is the central purpose of multilateralism: to constrain, discipline and civilize great power. Multilateralism is the strategy of the weak to constrain the strong, and it works only so long as the strong understand that these constraints relieve them of burdens that would otherwise be borne by the strong alone.

This brings me, finally, to Canada. How have we reacted to the slow erosion of American power and legitimacy? On the one hand, we have benefited. We have made a number of important strategic decisions in the past fifty years, all of which were opposed by the United States. These include the recognition of Cuba, followed by the recognition of China. Mr. Pearson disagreed with Lyndon Johnson over Vietnam. More recently, we have promoted the Landmine Treaty and the International Criminal Court in the teeth of U.S. opposition. Finally, of course, we refused to take part in the war in Iraq. Throughout this period, we have enhanced our independence and sovereignty by saying *no*. Indeed, throughout the past fifty years, the cost of saying no to the United States has gone down, not up, and Canada has taken advantage of this to enhance its freedom of action.

Yet while the relative decline of American legitimacy has benefited us, it has also imposed costs. It is beginning to dawn on us, for example, that our economy is tied to an economy which may not dominate the twenty-first century as it dominated the twentieth, and that if this is so, we had better improve our relations with the likely leaders: India and China. An America that is struggling to compete with these giants will result in a Canada struggling even more desperately.

Moreover, the neoconservative reaction to the crisis of American legitimacy—the unilateral turn—has directly weakened Canada's role in the world by weakening the multilateral institutions, like the UN, on which Canada depends for influence. Canada since 1945 has invested heavily in the logic of multilateralism, seeing in the elaboration of international law and international institutions a means to increase its own leverage in the world while also constraining the power of its more powerful neighbors. There is much to be said for this strategy: it has been in our national interest, as a middling power, and it has also been in the world's interest, since multilateral institutions share burdens, increase means of communication and reduce risks of conflict.

Canada has been dismayed by America's unilateral turn because it diminishes the influence and importance of the multilateral institutions in which we exercise such influence as we have: NATO, the UN, the OAS. The challenge for Canada is to reenergize these institutions and make them work so that America will see it's in its own interest to reinvest in them, too. In other words, America will not return to the multilateral order and exert leadership unless it is convinced that multilateral institutions actually work in its interest. They will only work in America's interest if she can see that such institutions share burdens that otherwise America would bear alone.

Afghanistan illustrates this point. NATO has stepped up to share America's burdens in nation-building and counterinsurgency since 2001. Canada has borne the brunt of the counterinsurgency struggle in Kandahar province. For many Canadians this is an unfamiliar and unwelcome kind of multilateralism. For most Canadians, peacekeeping under a UN flag is a happier—and certainly less risky—ideal of international engagement. Equally welcome is development activity under the auspices of UN agencies. In contrast to these ideas of multilateralism, the Afghan mission seems dangerous, difficult and even in conflict with Canadian ideals.

The problem is that the Afghan mission *is* multilateralism in action. We are there with the approval of the UN, under NATO command, and with the support of the elected Afghan government. If this isn't multilateralism, it is hard to know what is.

Moreover, it is multilateralism of the kind most likely to convince our American allies to reengage and reconnect with multilateralism itself. Put another way, if America is to be persuaded to turn away from unilateralism, if it is to be persuaded that multilateral constraints are in its best long-term interests, it is of some real importance that its best allies—and Canada counts among its best friends—demonstrate that they are willing to shoulder the more dangerous and risky aspects of multilateral commitment. If Canada does not rise to this challenge, Americans are only too likely to conclude that its allies believe in multilateralism only to the extent of doing the easy work—development and peacekeeping, while leaving the hard work to the Americans. This would make a nonsense of multilateralism itself, whose essence is equal burden-sharing by allies.

Canada thus has a considerable role in relegitimizing multilateralism in American eyes. It is in Canada's interest to do so, since a world where America lurches between unilateral aggression and isolationist withdrawal is not a safer world, but a more dangerous one. It is easy enough for Canadians to criticize Americans. It is even essential that we do so. What is unacceptable—a form of bad faith—is to criticize American unilateralism without being willing ourselves to shoulder our fair share of the burdens of multilateralism. We have a better chance of engaging the Americans in the construction of a multilateral world if we do our part of the hard work.

―――――――

Q: Can you comment on the idea that the position of the United States in the world is not a means or a goal but simply an outcome? The United States is, perhaps, the freest society in the world today and perhaps the freest society that the world has ever known. Could it be that, in comparison with Europe, with Islam, with China, because of the freedom and the liberty in the U.S., it will be in a position that it didn't desire, it didn't ask for, and in many ways is very reluctant to occupy?

A: I do think that there is something about American primacy since the Second World War that is directly related to the social model based on liberty. I don't think that any Canadian who thinks seriously about the United States can fail to be moved by Jefferson and Lincoln and Roosevelt. This was a political system that had global influence because it seemed to authentically define what a democracy was, as Lincoln gave it immortal expression. Some of the expansion of American power derived from the immense discursive, emotional, linguistic power of this political tradition and its example. It also depended crucially on America passing the test of the civil rights movement. It depended—for my generation—on watching a great society face up to the contradiction between "all men are created equal" and the palpable injustice of southern segregation. It depended on trying, in the Voting Rights Act of 1964 and 1965, to overcome that heritage and do it peacefully, without violence, with the greatest human rights campaign of the mid-twentieth century. So some of American primacy was derived from the power of moral example.

I'm not blind to America's defects. I'm not blind to the enormously large unmet racial agenda in the United States. But it has been a society that has tried occasionally to live by its creed.

Q: Is there a middle path between traditional liberal multilateralism and American unilateralism? If we're talking about trying to inject the rule of law in international affairs there are two things missing which are commonly associated with the rule of law as practiced within sovereign countries. One is a high degree of consensus on the basics of the system that we are going to live under. Second, the existence of a legitimate authority that everyone recognizes, that's going to enforce the laws. The middle path, therefore, may be rooted in trying to recreate those conditions at the international level; that is to say, of finding some degree of consensus amongst like-minded countries, and secondly, finding a sheriff. The middle path I want to propose is that the Americans are not hostile to the whole notion of working with other countries. What Americans are hostile to is the idea that they have to work with countries that may, in fact, wish them ill. They may be, however, amenable to an alliance of democratic countries where the American leadership is not viewed as being some terrible problem to be managed, but an asset to be exploited. Americans might be willing to work with some kind of a council of free nations, an alliance of democracies, but not with a system that gives France a veto because it happened to be on the winning side in the Second World War.

A: The first Bush administration was not as averse to multi-lateralism as the clichés about Iraq would have us believe. On foreign aid, on HIV/AIDS, on Sudan, on a lot of files, Colin Powell was very multilateral and very prepared to work with other countries when there was constancy of view, so there are all kinds of things that can be done with the Americans. That point is true. The question of whether you could get a kind of community of democracies to work with America and produce a new form of international legitimacy—I wish that was so. But you would still have France in the club, and France would still be as difficult in a club of democracies as it would at the UN Security Council. The unmet challenge here is that the UN is part of the problem and not part of the solution.

There is no way around that problem. A victor's club created in 1945, with the winners of a war that is now not within the direct-lived memory of most people in this room, is not the way to franchise legitimacy in the twenty-first century. It's impossible to explain why India isn't a member. It's impossible to explain why Germany isn't a member. It's impossible to explain why Brazil isn't a member, right? It just doesn't make any sense. It's also impossible, in my judgment, to defend the veto. If you want to refranchise international legitimacy, you've got to change the institution that does the legitimizing. Nobody is prepared to step up to the challenge.

We've got a situation in which, whenever the United States has to use force, it will step outside the system if it can't get what it wants, and that's where we are now.

Q: Has the American thrust into the Middle East and September 11, in a strange way, caused a change in dialectic that moves us back to Louis St. Laurent, who said, as Foreign Minister, that the principles of Canadian foreign policy are based on three words: freedom, liberty and making the world safe for democracy? And in your view as someone who has been a Canadian export, rather than a resident of this country, is there anything that makes it more sensible for us to put our money into the things you've talked about rather than just sending money to the democratic presidential candidate?

A: Somebody mentioned the role of America in advancing democracy and freedom, and said that that was consonant with Canadian foreign policy goals. It's not a fashionable thing to say, but the fact is there are more functioning democracies in the world now, according to Freedom House, than at any other time in the history of the world. And some of that depends on the fact that the global power with primacy in the world is the United States. Canada has played a very important role in democracy promotion. We all think, obviously, that we're the most corrupt and degraded political system the world has ever known. In fact, in comparable terms, if you look at the transparency index, Canada is one of the best-governed, least corrupt countries in the world, in a ranking of

190. It doesn't mean we're saints. It doesn't mean we're terrific. But peace, order and good government is something we know an awful lot about and we've played a discreet role in exporting those experiences.

When I was in Croatia in 1992 I met a Saskatoon traffic cop from the RCMP who was escorting Croatians into Serbian territory and back; saving lives, making family reunification possible. An ordinary Canadian doing a job that everybody in this room ought to be proud of. She said it was the greatest thing she had ever done in her life. Beats writing traffic tickets on a cold highway in Saskatchewan, that's for sure. Ever since the Second World War, Canadian foreign policy has been linked to democracy maintenance and democracy promotion, to peace, order and good government.

If you go to northern Iraq, as I did in March with an old school buddy of mine, Bob Rae, who works for the Forum of Federations, and you sit in Irbil and you talk to the Kurdish leadership, you might think Canadians don't have much to say about Iraq. And yet we've got a huge amount to say about Iraq because Canada knows more about federalism than any other country in the world. We've got the wounds to prove it. If Iraq has got a chance of avoiding civil war, it has to get a federal constitution. Canada is a country that has a lot to say about federalism but we don't tell our story very well. We've made a multilingual, bilingual, multinational, blah-de-blah, aboriginal rights country hold together for 130 years. It's a good story. We have something to say that is very different from the Americans on this. God help Iraq if they adopt American federalism. They've got a chance to make it if they adopt something like asymmetrical, Rube Goldberg, Canadian federalism. But they haven't got a chance if it's an American model. So Canada has something quite specific to say and we'd better stump up the money to say it because Canadians can play a direct role in advising smart Iraqis about how to avoid civil war.

Q: It's really interesting that the word "fascism" is cropping up in the United States, but it's not necessarily the word I would have used to describe the politics of the United States right now. Not that it matters what Canadians think, or France thinks. What Americans think matters and only an educated American population can make good decisions.

A: There are people who are worried about American fascism. I guess by "fascism" they mean a kind of authoritarian populism, based on religious evangelical mobilization, but I just don't see it. I'm a Lester B. Pearson, Pierre Trudeau, tax and spend, civil libertarian, gay-marriage liberal. But the reality is we were beat fair and square in November 2004. We were beaten by a better political campaign and a better candidate. Yes, folks—a better retail politician beat us twice. The other team had a better grasp of the American political vocabulary, a better grasp of the language of values, a better grasp of the language of American political traditions, and they beat us square. It was a political victory. It's not a cultural victory. It's not an eternal victory. We weren't beat by fascism. We were beat by good, down and dirty politics. And we weren't beat by the power of money. Democrats had as much money as the Republicans. We can't blame nefarious monopoly capitalism. We had as much money at the table as they did and we couldn't do the job.

You said what Canadians think doesn't matter. With deepest respect, I think this is wrong. The whole burden of my talk is that Canadians are far too obsessed with American power. The greatest achievements of our political tradition were created by people entirely unafraid of American power. Lester Pearson created a medicare system inspired by Saskatchewan and the CCF and his own intuitions about what was right. Pierre Trudeau created a *Charter of Rights and Freedoms*. They created political space at the top of North America and they did the business. In the process, they solidified an absolutely distinctive political tradition.

What we say matters to ourselves, and what we say to other people matters. Canada matters—it's a G8 country. Canada has international capital all over the place. If we start into a mindset that says nothing we do in our political system matters, we'll stop voting. We'll stop investing. We'll stop caring. Our political system matters intensely, and what we say matters intensely, to ourselves and to other people. Why would I come out on a Thursday night, to a small provincial town in North America, unless I thought talking to Canadians and being with Canadians mattered intensely? One symptom of the psychological sickness of being Canadian is a sense that our discourse doesn't matter relative to the big political discourse down south. We've got to get out of that headspace because we wouldn't have done the great things we've done if we thought that.

Q: Perhaps there is another hyperpower: China. How do you feel the United States will react to it? How you think China might behave and where does Canada fit into that equation?

A: A guy who works for one of the big New York firms—and who also worked for Kofi Annan—was in Shanghai and he sent me an e-mail right in the middle of Iraq. He said, when you look at the world from Shanghai, where the towers are mushrooming every five minutes, where there's a kind of din and a cacophony of building all around, and you look at rates of growth rates in China, when you look at a population of one billion, you are looking at an enormous hegemonic power. The Chinese sit there and watch their imperial rival tied down in a war in Iraq and it looks pretty good. That is to say, if you step back from where we are, on the north of the 49th parallel, obsessed with our relationship with this difficult country, and look more globally, in twenty-five years our children will be astonished at our obsession with the United States. They will be struck by how little we understood about the emerging global power in Asia and will be struck that we didn't make contact with China and India early enough. Most of all, they will be astonished that we did nothing about global warming and that we sat here obsessed with American power and didn't use our capacities at this moment to make change in Asia.

In other words, we've got America on our mind. It's bad for Canada. It's bad for our political imagination. It's shutting us down. We've got to think big thoughts. Our greatest leaders—Trudeau and Pearson—thought big, big thoughts, thoughts specific to this country that turned out to have enormous global resonance. I hope we stay true to that vision of ourselves because we're not in Bush league.

U.S. EMPIRE, OR
UNIMULTIPOLAR WORLD?

SAMUEL P. HUNTINGTON
JANUARY 20, 2005

Professor Samuel P. Huntington, author of The Clash of
Civilizations *and perhaps the most influential political scientist of
his generation, argues unequivocally that an American empire is
nothing more than a myth. Instead, he puts forth the theory that the
post–Cold War world has become a "unimultipolar" world, in
which the U.S., as the only superpower, must come to terms with
regional powers who believe they have a stake in their own areas,
and who have come to resent outside interference. It's a situation, he
argues, that has made the U.S.'s desire to export democracy both
foolish and dangerous.*

My central argument is that an American empire doesn't exist. It is a myth. The fact that people believe in this myth has, however, some not-good consequences. Because of the belief in this myth by both Americans and non-Americans, we are moving in a direction in which, if current trends continue, Iraq will be the first in a series of incidents that have disastrous consequences.

In order to talk about an empire, one must define empire. If one looks at the literature on empires, the usual definition is that empire is the rule exercised by one nation or one people over other peoples. Clearly, the United States has not been much of an empire throughout its history. They did have a few colonies at one time in the Philippines and a few other places, but they did not exercise direct rule over other people. More recent theorists and commentators on empire, however, have broadened the definition far beyond that which I provided, to include the ability to shape events in other societies in a significant way. One of the interesting things about the thinking on the concept of an American empire is that during the Cold War, "American Empire" was a phrase used largely by liberal critics of the United States to denounce it: "You're creating an empire. You're imperialistic and obviously that's very bad."

One of the astonishing things in the past decade, however, has been the extent to which the concept of America having an empire has been adopted so enthusiastically by people who are labeled neoconservatives. We now have neo-conservative enthusiasm for the idea of an American empire. I don't know what my old friend and former student Bill Kristol said when he spoke, but he is one of the most articulate enthusiasts of the American empire. So we have a peculiar situation in which liberals find it hard to challenge the idea of an American empire because the neoconservatives say, "We should go out and reform the world, promote democracy and human rights and reshape the world basically in the American image." Liberals just do not know how to deal with that sort of conservatism.

I think that the idea of an American empire is dangerous because it doesn't describe reality and because it leads to activities such as the invasion of Iraq, which have very unfortunate consequences. The concept of American empire does not describe reality, even in this much broader sense.

To the extent that America may have had an empire in this broader sense, it had a very incomplete semi-empire during the Cold War years, when America was the leader of a coalition of countries which we euphemistically called the free world. However, many of those countries were dictatorships of one sort or another, and, because we were protecting these countries from the threats of the Soviet Union and communism, they were dependent on the United States and, hence, the United States could exercise a great deal of control over them, and often did.

With the collapse of the Soviet Union and the end of the Cold War, however, the power of the United States also has declined momentously. Now, people always say, "Well, you're the only superpower and therefore you don't have the opposition from the Soviet Union and therefore you can do anything you want." But that is simply not the case because you can only exercise authority and influence over other countries if you can get them to go along, if they need you in one way or another. Countries all over the world now no longer need the United States to provide their security as they did during the Cold War.

The idea that the European Union would have evolved in the way in which it has during the past decade or so would have been unthinkable during the Cold War, when the United States was crucial to providing security for Germany and France. Now, that is no longer the case. They don't need the United States, and U.S. control over them, as well as over many other countries, clearly has gone down dramatically.

How can we think about the dynamics of global politics, given these circumstances? In my book, *The Clash of Civilizations and the Remaking of World Order*, I emphasized the extent to which culture and religion play increasingly important roles in shaping the way in which countries act, in their friendships and antagonisms. That fact has been validated in a number of very unfortunate developments since I first advanced the idea in 1993.

Power is always relevant to what goes on in the world and to interstate relations. The structure of global power now is very different from what it was during the Cold War. I will point to some of the implications of this dramatic change, which I think is equally important with the shift from the emphasis on secular political ideologies during the Cold War to the cultural and religious factors that are more important now.

It is useful to think of the current structure of global power in terms of four levels. First, the United States is indeed the only superpower with overwhelming dominance in virtually every category of power, whether it is military, economic, technological, cultural or diplomatic. The United States stands alone at level one in this structure of global power.

Second, there are, at level two, perhaps six or eight major regional powers. These would include the European Union, meaning basically the German and France condominium in Europe; Russia; China; India; Brazil in Latin America; Israel in the Middle East; Iran in the Persian Gulf; Indonesia in Southeast Asia; and probably South Africa in Africa. These are powers that don't have the same global sweep as the United States does, but still like to think that they should exercise the shaping influence within their particular regions of the world.

Third, a large number of secondary regional powers exist in every region. These are countries which are less influential within the region or in the world than the major regional powers. Some of them are clearly very important countries, but still have to orient their attitudes and thinking to their relationship with the major regional powers. These include the United Kingdom, in Europe; Poland; Ukraine; Uzbekistan in the Russian sphere; Pakistan; Japan; Argentina; and various other countries. That's just a small selection of secondary regional powers.

At the fourth level is everybody else. Some countries are important for one reason or another, but don't quite play the same role in shaping global politics.

In a world in which there is an empire, the imperial power is able to resolve major international issues on its own with little consultation or help from other actors, states or otherwise. In what we might call a multipolar world, countries do interact with each other, but not on the basis of complete equality as was the case in Europe for several centuries. Countries shifted their alliances, varied their patterns of cooperation and conflict from one period to another. The dominant pattern was one in which countries combined to prevent any one power from becoming too powerful. Hence, a balance of power emerged. In the European system, you had to have a coalition of countries that was prepared to deal effectively with any single international issue.

What do we have now in this four-level structure of global politics that I have described? I call this structure a unimultipolar system, which is an extremely awkward term. That description does not have any of the rhetorical clout of the "end of history" or the "clash of civilizations." If anybody can come up with a zingier label for it, I would be grateful, but it seems to me that we are now in a unimultipolar world.

The United States cannot, by itself, dictate what goes on. The United States needs the cooperation of some of the major regional powers to accomplish anything effectively in world affairs.

On the other hand, the United States, as the only superpower, is generally able to veto international actions proposed by any coalition of other major actors. This creates a new natural pattern of antagonism emerging in the world. During the Cold War, when there were two superpowers, it was virtually inevitable that they would be rivals while trying to extend their influence in different parts of the world. This rivalry was reinforced by the fact that each was trying to promote a universalist ideology throughout the world.

In the new structure of power, a natural antagonism exists between the superpower and the major regional powers. The United States thinks it has, and in large part it does have, significant interests in every part of the world, and it wants to promote those interests. It wants to shape what goes on in every region in the world. Each of the major regional powers, however, thinks that it should be able to shape what goes on in its part of the world and clearly resents the efforts of the United States to do that and, hence, antagonism. I do not think, however, that any sort of violent conflict is likely.

In some cases, there will be effective cooperation. There has been effective cooperation between the United States and some major regional powers. But that is rare. The natural pattern, as we can see developing in relations between the United States and the major regional powers, is one of differences of interest and conflict of one sort or another.

There may be exceptions to this. One exception was when, after September 11, the United States and several of the major regional powers suddenly woke up to the threat of terrorism. I think President Bush, in coming up with a global war on terror as the goal and as the need at the moment, scored a tremendous political success because this aligned the

United States with several of these other major regional powers. Putin immediately said, "Of course, we're waging a war on terror." And the Chinese, Indians and Israelis agreed.

For a brief moment, you had the beginnings of a global coalition. It did not last long because the idea of a war on terror was also a figment of imagination. There were several different wars that governments were waging against insurgencies and terrorist tactics. You don't fight a war on terror. Terrorism is a tactic. You may fight a war against the people who use that tactic, but they are the enemy and clearly the enemy is different in all of these situations. Now the differences have come to the fore and the idea of a war on terrorism as a great crusade of the civilized world has been shown to be unsupportable. There are many differences that are emerging between the United States and the major regional powers.

There is a third level of actors: the secondary regional powers. What are their interests? One underlying interest is not to be dominated by the big brother next door, by the major power in their region. Hence, they share an interest in working with the United States against the big brothers in the form of the major regional powers.

Think back over the past decade, and recall the ways in which the relations between the United States and the secondary regional powers have improved tremendously or been reinforced. In some cases, the U.S. had good relations with them. These have all been reinforced now because there is a common concern about the major regional powers.

In some cases, these closer relationships between the U.S. and the secondary regional powers are the result of other factors that also play a role—political ideology, most notably. There is also a basis for cooperation simply in the structure of global politics. We've seen this in the reaffirmation and intensification of the special relationship between the U.S. and Britain; in the tremendous strengthening that has occurred in the past decade of the U.S. alliance with Japan; and in the shift in U.S. attitudes toward South America, where in the past Brazil was the South American country that worked most closely with the United States, sending troops on occasion to fight with American forces, and where Argentina was our traditional enemy.

Now those relationships have been reversed. Brazil is leading the opposition to the U.S. in South America by trying to develop Mercosur as an alternative to the U.S.-proposed Western free-trade area, while Argentina has become closer to the U.S.

With respect to Europe, of course, and Eurasia, the best friend the U.S. has in Europe, with the possible exception of Britain, is Poland. Poland is a country that feels threatened by two major regional powers and, over the centuries, has suffered occupation and partition by the Germans and the Russians. Poland is an enthusiastic supporter of the United States. The United States has also developed reasonably close relations with countries like Georgia and Uzbekistan.

One can see the significance of these alignments if one looks at the attitudes that governments took toward the launching of the war in Iraq. All of the countries that I would call major regional powers, with the notable exception of Israel, opposed and condemned it. Most of the secondary regional powers supported the war and provided troops in varying degrees. The principal providers of troops to fight in the war included Britain but also Poland and Ukraine, who sent not just token numbers, but relatively large numbers of troops.

Other countries did join in—Italy and Spain. Spain, however, has now pulled out and probably other countries will pull out. If you look at the initial lineups, there is a striking correlation with the role and place of countries in the global power structure that I have described.

Given this situation, the first question a scholar of international relations would ask would be, why haven't the major regional powers formed a strong coalition to contain and limit U.S. power? Obviously, they each have their differences with the U.S. with respect to what goes on in their region. They want to limit U.S. power. Why don't they get together and form a coalition? This, after all, is the way in which European politics classically operate.

There have been some efforts in that direction. Every year or so the leaders from countries like Iran and India and Russia and China get together and issue declarations condemning hegemony and calling for a movement toward a multipolar world, but so far those are just declarations.

There has been significant cooperation between these countries, most notably in that China has provided information on nuclear weapons and nuclear weapons technology to other countries. There are various other ways in which they have been cooperating with each other in an effort to constrain U.S. power. Overall, things have not gone exactly the way in which one might predict if one looked back at the patterns in European history.

Why is this? First, the classical pattern of balance of power politics in Europe involved countries which were basically within the same civilization. They understood each other and they understood the limits and the purposes of their actions. They did not want any one country to dominate.

Now, the coalition to establish a balance of power would have to involve countries with very different cultures and outlooks, such as Russia, China, India, France and Germany. That is much more difficult to do.

Second, there is a significant difference in the incentives that the United States can offer these countries to cooperate. In particular, the United States has leverage on the less developed countries because it can offer them economic aid and military assistance, facilitate their entry into international organizations, and invite their leaders to the White House, all of which are meaningful for less developed countries. Those incentives do not mean much to the Western European powers, to France and Germany. Hence there is a discrepancy in the ability of the United States to induce the potential members of an anti-U.S. coalition to refrain from joining such a coalition.

Third, perhaps it is too early for such a coalition to form. Maybe it will take time for it to develop. Another major difference from the European experience is that the challenge or threat that the United States poses to these other powers clearly is not the threat of military invasion. In Europe, invasion usually was a threat. One country invaded another country and the additional countries rallied to the defense of the victim. Clearly, the acute threat of a military invasion is not something that is significant at the moment. Now the threat is that of limitation of action, coercion from the superior power of the United States, which will only have an effect over a period of time.

Finally, there are rivalries among the major regional powers, and several of them may want to maintain good relations with the United States in order to get its help in a rivalry with a neighboring major power, such as India against China or Russia against China. In the long run it is possible that some more substantial and lasting coalition may emerge to counter American power.

Even in the current situation, the United States has not been very successful in achieving what it has announced as its major objectives, such as preventing nuclear proliferation. Proliferation obviously continues. A variety of states have been working on creating at least the potential to develop nuclear weapons. Iran undoubtedly will have nuclear weapons at some point in the next three or four years. They keep promising that they will open themselves up to inspection but they always back away from doing so.

It is natural for any country that considers itself the major power in its region to want nuclear weapons. Nuclear weapons are the symbol of a nation's power. I do not think nuclear weapons are going to be used by a state in any war in the future, but they are the symbol of a nation's power. When a major regional power like India got nuclear weapons, that fact just encouraged Pakistan to demonstrate that it had nuclear weapons, too. So if a major regional power gets nuclear weapons, some secondary regional powers are going to want those capabilities also.

That is a losing wicket as far as the United States is concerned. Certainly, the United States has not been successful in a significant way in the past decade in promoting democratization around the world. It has also not been successful in gaining significant, meaningful support for the Iraq war. There is also a general, broader feeling of anti-Americanism throughout the world; the view that the United States is just too powerful and has to be cut down to size.

These factors all are at work in a variety of ways as we see efforts by many countries to change the structure of global politics from what I have awkwardly called a unimultipolar world into a truly multipolar world. If one looks at the various trends and developments, one could conclude that that is the way in which the world is moving. Both the world and the United States will probably be much better off once we get there.

———

Q: In light of your own thinking about where the United States is these days, and where the United States identity is moving in terms of all of the cracks and fissures that are developing in the country, where is the American empire headed?

A: It's obviously very hard to say because there are so many factors affecting it. As I argue in my latest book, *Who Are We?* there are all sorts of developments going on in the United States which, if continued, will have the effect of decreasing American national identity. We already see the extent to which our politics have become polarized in ways they certainly weren't going back as far as I can remember, and that's pretty far. The divisions in our society—economic, political and cultural—are increasing. These were briefly patched over after September 11, but I think the forces promoting these divisions are there and, hence, it's hard to say what's going to win out.

At the moment, the neoconservatives are certainly in charge, but I don't think they're going to be able to continue that pattern for very long. The idea that we might invade Iran, which is talked about presently, is so preposterous that it can only be rooted in a total ignorance of Persian Gulf countries and cultures, one which exceeds the ignorance that existed when we went into Iraq. If we do pursue that sort of line, there will be an immense reaction against it from the American public. One of the things I demonstrated in my book is the extent to which the attitudes of the American public about foreign affairs differ significantly from the attitudes of leading segments of the American elite.

The American public, as every comparative public opinion poll comparing the attitudes of forty or more countries shows, is among the most nationalistic and patriotic in the world. Certain segments of the American elite are in the process of being denationalized as a result of globalization. Business people, professional people, academics, journalists and others can pursue their careers anywhere and so they lose their identification with their country. There have been some very interesting studies carried out, where elites in major international corporations and foundations like the Ford Foundation are interviewed, and the prevailing attitude that these people express is, "I'm a global citizen. I happen to have an American passport but I consider myself a citizen of the world."

You can see increasing differences in the attitudes of these elites on the one hand, and the American public on the other. At some point, there could be a more nationalistic reaction against some of the foreign policies that have been pushed by the elites. Certainly, I think, as everyone recognizes, NAFTA would never get through Congress now.

Q: To what degree do you believe that causes like a commitment to individual rights and freedoms or free markets can align U.S. foreign policy with other sane human beings who are committed to similar policies, regardless of the countries they currently inhabit? Is it possible to support democratic versus dictatorial regimes so that you don't have to tolerate

Iran getting nuclear weapons just because you're opposed to American hegemony?

A: I think political ideologies and economic theories and approaches to economics do play a role. Certainly, they have facilitated George Bush's relationships in the past, at least, with the leaders in Italy and Spain and other countries who had somewhat comparable views. I wouldn't play down the extent to which those considerations are a factor. In the longer run, I think whatever changes occur in the political tendency or economic philosophy that is dominant in a country will be perceived by leaders largely in geopolitical terms. If you look at the relationships that I've spoken about tonight in terms of different places in the power structure, the really critical ones (where there is a danger of serious clashes) tend to be those where differences in the stages in the power structure coincide with differences in culture.

It is often said that the United States should go out and export democracy or free markets to other countries, but I think this is something to be avoided. We can certainly support the groups in those countries that want to move in that direction, but I think that is all we can do. The idea that we're going to be able to impose our rather peculiar view of democracy and of economic liberalism on other countries seems to me to be a very dangerous fallacy.

IS WHAT'S GOOD FOR AMERICA GOOD FOR THE WORLD?

JOHN LUKACS
MARCH 10, 2005

Historian John Lukacs, renowned author of bestselling books on Churchill, Hitler and Stalin, used his lecture as an opportunity to reexamine two centuries of American foreign policy. He argues that although the United States is no longer an imperial power, it was once—and that the desire for international influence present in the waning years of the nineteenth century helped to create a trend toward "universalism" that is still at play today. This "universalistic" impulse says that what is good for America (including democracy) is good for the world. Lukacs is highly critical of this assumption, and he concludes that it can do great harm—both outside the United States and to the political discourse taking place within the country's own borders.

A re Americans imperialists?" This is a difficult and serious question. The first problem is the very word "imperialist." Centuries ago "imperialist" meant supporters of emperors. After the 1870s, it began to mean people who favor empires. Thus imperialism is not necessarily pro-aristocratic; it may be a democratic inclination. It is discernable, too, within the tendencies of the American national character.

Americans were nationalists from their very beginnings. This is often the case with very young nations who wish to find a certain kind of identity and take pride in the fact that they established themselves. Popular sentiment in the U.S. was not always in accord with the leaders, especially not of the founders. There has been a duality in the history of American foreign relations exemplified by John Quincy Adams, a man who was probably the greatest American secretary of state in the two hundred years of the republic. On one hand, he forced the Spanish to agree to a hard treaty that extended America's frontiers. Yet in 1821 he said in a speech in accord with the one where he drafted the Monroe Doctrine, "We are friends of liberty all over the world, but we do not go abroad in search for monsters to destroy." Has anyone in the present administration listened to, or ever heard, John Quincy Adams' words?

Speaking of American political history, we ought to make a distinction between public opinion and popular sentiment.

In a democracy, much of a nation's discourse is dictated or governed by public opinion. But these terms have been confused in the last hundred years and especially nowadays. When we speak of public opinion polls, what they try to ascertain or measure or put into figures is really popular sentiment. Popular sentiment and public opinion are not the same things. "Public" is not "popular" and "opinion" is not "sentiment." Popular sentiment is an inclination, a powerful tendency not always clearly ascertainable or expressed. Public opinion in the nineteenth century mostly meant readers of newspapers by the middle classes, a relative minority then in a democratic nation such as England.

This discrepancy between popular sentiment and public opinion may be detected throughout American history. We can see it as early as the 1840s when an Irish-American demagogue coined the term "manifest destiny;"—the idea that the United States had a manifest destiny to rule the entire North American continent. At the same time when the Manifest Destiny slogan became very popular, it was overruled by the president and by the more educated kind of public opinion that existed in the United States—the same people who, in the 1840s, decided to accept the division of the American and British-Canadian empires on the 49th parallel.

This is one example where the interests of the American state did not quite accord to the inclinations of popular sentiment. This happened several times throughout the nineteenth century. Some of it involved Canada. It also involved Cuba. There were important popular movements to liberate or invade the island and add it to the union. The majority of the southern states, who otherwise spoke of states' rights and independence, were in favor of annexing and invading Cuba and sometimes even parts of Mexico that remained after 1848. The discrepancy between popular sentiment and public opinion may be seen throughout the Lincoln administration and its relationship with Great Britain during the Civil War. Then, in 1898, there was a change. American public opinion, particularly the educated opinion, had a strong tendency to ask, "Why does not the United States also need an empire?" just as the British, French, Germans, Italians and Belgians had theirs. The Spanish-American War of 1898 was a result of powerful pressures created by both public opinion and popular sentiment. Popular sentiment supported the war, but so did highly educated Americans such as John Hay and Theodore Roosevelt. This was a great change in the entire history of the world. No matter what Copernicus and Magellan discovered geographically, politically speaking the world did not become round until 1900. For the first time, two great non-European imperial powers were willing to extend their sway across large seas beyond their immediate reach. They were the United States and Japan. That's when the world became politically round. What the United States and Japan did or did not do between 1900 and 1914 had a very important effect on Europe.

People speak much today of American "exceptionalism." True, but not true enough. American exceptionalism is one of those terms that confuses things, rather than clarifies them. Something happened after the war of 1898 and before the First World War, when American "exceptionalism" or "nationalism" or nascent "imperialism" (whatever you want to call it), turned into a kind of universalism. A universalism that said what's good for America is not only good for the world, but it's made the world safe for democracy. But the question before us and before our descendants may be the very opposite: "Can democracy be made safe for the world?" It is a question that Alexis de Tocqueville would have understood, but Woodrow Wilson did not.

Wilson's universalism was defeated in the election of 1920 by a majority of Americans who ever since then have been called, rather inaccurately, "isolationists." But it is perhaps in the nature of democratic society itself, especially of Americans, to posses a kind of split-mindedness. For few of the American isolationists were really isolationists. Beginning in 1919 and into the 1920s they opposed, with some reason, American involvement in Europe, yet were extreme imperialists when it came to the Caribbean, to Nicaragua and even to parts of the Far East. Franklin Roosevelt in 1939 and 1941 and thereafter was sometimes unduly cautious about isolationist opinion. But what is very interesting and telling is that most American isolationists, many of them who in 1941 and before were bitterly opposed to the United States giving help to Britain and getting involved in the war against Germany, by 1947 became the loudest advocates of a crusade against the Soviet Union. And what was so "isolationist" about that? These are examples of a certain kind of American split-mindedness that characterizes American popular sentiment and much of American politics till this day. This divide is evident in its choice of words within American political terminology.

There were American presidents and statesmen, and not only John Quincy Adams, who were much more conservative than the popular sentiment of their day. But until about 1950 the word "conservative" was avoided and eschewed by all Americans. Senator Robert A. Taft, idol of the present conservatives in the right-wing Republican Party, in 1950 said, "I am not a conservative. I am an old-fashioned liberal." By 1960, "conservative" began to be an acceptable word in America. By 1980, more Americans identified themselves as conservatives than as liberals. This is a tectonic change of great importance. Yet most American conservatives don't want to conserve much, if anything. They are not conservatives, not in their domestic policy, and not in their foreign policy. What this means is that the Republican Party became the populist party in America. The "populists" who, a hundred years ago, were on the left wing of the Democratic Party have to a large extent vanished. Their descendants have become Republicans. The Republican Party, in every sense of the word, has become populist, demonstrating the decline of democracy, something against which the founders argued and legislated and wrote a constitution to avoid.

We are told that in a democracy "the people" speak. But in reality the people do not speak. There are men and women who speak in the name of the people—and that is another issue, a complicated one, not equivalent to true democratic reality.

This suggests another problem involving majority choice. Many conservative opponents of democracy have feared the tyranny of the majority. But what is "the" majority?

In the United States, there are hard minorities and soft majorities. And it is in the capacity of hard minorities to exercise an influence on popular sentiments way beyond their numbers and also way beyond their intellectual propriety. It is the older political categories, "right" and "left," and especially "conservative" and "liberal," that have lost most of their meaning. Consider Woodrow Wilson, who was defeated in 1920 but now, for almost a century, Herbert Hoover, Franklin Roosevelt, Richard Nixon, Ronald Reagan and George W. Bush—all different political leaders (four of them Republicans)—have been Wilsonians. And because they are Wilsonians and universalists, this is a very difficult and complicated problem for the American people. American universalism can do a great amount of harm not only outside the U.S. but also to standards of honesty and decency within the political discourse of the American people themselves. To quote Machiavelli's *The Prince,* "Fortune smiles on the well situated, the enterprising and the courageous, but not on the overconfident, the reckless and those who willfully ignore the past."

———————

Q: When you suggest that there is a divorce between "the people" and the people who speak for the people, unlike the old days when Thomas Jefferson was writing, "we, the people," this strikes me as being kind of a thought about the past being so much better than the present, but the present being where we live. So, practically speaking, if you have these concerns about American universalism, could you say one charitable thing about it?

A: The charitable thing about American universalism is American generosity. Americans are generous people, very often thoughtlessly. As Dr. Johnson said, "intentions must be judged by acts." Two things must be understood, however. Generosity with your goods, or with your ability, is a very fine human attribute. But there is something greater and that is magnanimity—the willingness to give something not of your goods but of yourself. It means seeing something in your opponent and your enemy that is also deeply human. That is not the mark of any kind of universalism.

The other problematic thing about generosity is the relationship between justice and truth. This is not only an American problem, but it is also a very American problem. There is an American tendency of wanting to spread justice all over the world. Spreading justice can destroy the world. It is Captain Ahab in *Moby Dick*, who destroys his crew because he wants to get even with the white whale. Justice can be destructive. In a way, this is the great fault of liberalism—to think that it is the destiny of modern man to eliminate injustice all over the world. In this respect, liberalism has triumphed. There is no more slavery. We have emancipated people, emancipated slaves, people of color, rising power of universal suffrage and universal education. But all over the world today, in the United States as much as anywhere else, there hang the black clouds of untruth. Untruth by our mass production of so-called information, entertainment and propaganda. Truth is of a deeper order than justice and any kind of universalism confuses truth and justice. In fact, universalism puts the emphasis on justice over truth.

This is the same difference as that between generosity and magnanimity, and in order to be preachy, if you look at the New Testament, Christ never promised justice. He said, "I am the truth."

Q: Canadians tend to be very self-absorbed and perhaps this is why we not more actively involved in Iraq.

A: I'm very impressed by what the Canadians did in two world wars but I think this is also inseparable from their then-feeling, encompassing the people, regarding the mother country. It was a kind of loyalty Canadians fulfilled to the utmost and I'm very impressed by that.

I don't know much about Canadian self-absorption, but I don't think it's such a bad thing to be self-absorbed. To be self-absorbed means that, to some extent, you know your own limits. Self-absorption involves some kind of self-knowledge, some ability to look in the mental mirror and say, "I

can do this," or "I'm going to do this and not that." I don't
think this is a very bad thing. It is, by and large, a very
admirable thing. The great trouble is that we are preaching
freedom all over the world but, as the Greeks knew, it's more
difficult to be free than not to be free. Freedom should not
come from a government or from a church or society.
Freedom should be the ability to write your own rules,
which means establishing your own restrictions. Self-
absorption is not identical with this but I don't think it's
always contradictory.

Q: You're a historian and not a futurist, but looking around
at the influence of the United States in the Middle East—
where the vision of Iraq has consequences which are
critiqued left and right, where no one's quite sure what's to
happen next and all the while there seems to be a rise in
civil society agitation in places that didn't have it before—
what would you say to the Bush administration? You've
critiqued the administration tonight. If they were to actually take the whole picture, the history that they should
learn from, and look at where they are now, what would
you have them do?

A: History does not repeat itself. Historians repeat themselves, but I will try not to do that. Life is full of unintended
consequences, you know. I was bitterly opposed to the war
against Iraq but maybe something good is going to come out
of it. I do not know. I'll tell you what bothered me about this
war and about Iraq in the very beginning. It is something I

cannot prove but I'm very suspicious about. There were American presidents in the past who wanted to go to war. Polk wanted to go to war against Mexico. Lincoln wanted to go to war against the south. McKinley wanted to go to war. Wilson wanted to go to war. Roosevelt wanted to go to war, all for reasons that they thought were in the utmost interest of the nation. I think this is the first president who wanted to go to war with a dictator to be popular.

Q: At the risk of sounding overly deterministic and perhaps materialist, it's also suggested through history that empires who may, accidentally or by design, arrive at the state of empire feel that they have strategic interests to protect and it's possible that at various times they might use popular opinion or popular sentiment in order to justify the defense of those strategic interests.

In general, one assumes an empire is an empire because it can project power on a grander scale. One could speculate about what might be the strategic interests in the American context: non-nuclear proliferation, safety from terrorism and security of energy supply. These are three things that come to mind. To what extent can popular sentiment or even public opinion be swayed or serve as instruments in the protection of "strategic interest," in the current context?

A: Strategic interests are perhaps easy to define, but they are not always the motive powers of government. I think in this president's decision to go to war with Iraq, strategic interests or oil interests were a very minor element. Every decision has more than one cause. They are multicausal but some causes are more important than others. This war was popular with people, of whom the majority could not find Iraq on the map.

I don't think strategic interests always exist. Defining strategic interests is complicated when it involves measuring the possible sale of a policy against its popularity. In a democratic age the very structure of events is more complicated than in previous ages. How and why something happens has become a very complex thing and involves all kinds of elements. It goes completely against the prevalent philosophy of materialism. It means a constant, steady increase of the influence of mind into matter.

Q: I put it to you that at the supreme moment of American importance in the world, just coming to the end of the Second World War—when the United States had half of the gross product of the world because of the destruction of so many other economies, and greater air and naval power than all other countries in the world combined, and a colossal army of three hundred divisions, and was on the verge of a nuclear monopoly—that they showed great magnanimity in putting forward Roosevelt as president, Truman as vice-president, Marshall as chairman of the combined Allied military chiefs and, as theater commanders, Douglas MacArthur, Eisenhower and Chester Nimitz. No country in history has ever demonstrated such a high level of leadership at anything remotely approaching so critical a point and those men— well, Roosevelt died, but the rest of them, largely following his example—showed great magnanimity.

There have been fluctuations but, in general, I think America has been a magnanimous country. On the matter of George W. Bush going to war for popularity, I don't believe that. I think Bush went to war because he was convinced that the Arab world in particular, and much of the Muslim world generally, was going to be a breeding ground for instability for an indefinite period unless the Arab self-perception of centuries and centuries of retreat could be reversed. The only way to do it was to establish one of the major Arab countries as a place where there was not a perfect democracy, like the state of Connecticut or the province of Ontario, but some power sharing and some reasonable distribution of the wealth of the country. I think that the United States is essentially magnanimous, with failings of course, but generally magnanimous. And certainly it bears comparison in that regard with any other leading country in world history since the rise of the nation state. I think you rather shortchange your president when you claim he went to war for popularity. Frankly, I think McKinley went to war for popularity, but why not? Why shouldn't he?

A: Well, you raise two arguments and I quite agree with your first. I think the United States really acted both generously and magnanimously after 1945, when it had all the power in the world. But don't forget that these were Democrats. Eisenhower, in as late as 1948, was flirting with the idea of running as a Democrat. Don't forget that in 1946, the Republicans made great gains in the congressional elections with the slogan, "Had enough?" And by 1950 and 1952, the

Democrats and the liberals are in decline because the Republican Party and the rising conservative movement in the United States accuses Truman and Marshall and Acheson and those people of being too soft on communism and this was populism of a very cheap and a very bad sort. I agree with you that the American attitude after the Second World War, both popular and public and governmental, was not only generous but, in many ways, magnanimous. That has passed.

PART II

THE UNITED STATES IN THE MIDDLE EAST

THE AMERICAN
MILITARY AS NGO

ROBERT KAPLAN
SEPTEMBER 8, 2005

Robert Kaplan, the well-known journalist and national correspondent for the Atlantic Monthly, *has been embedded with the American forces both around the world and in Iraq with the 1st Battalion of the 5th Marine Regiment in Fallujah. Here, Kaplan argues that exporting democracy to the Middle East will create a period of instability that could last for ten to fifteen years. During that period, he believes, a sustained effort will be required to ensure that humanitarian needs are met. It is a job for which the American military is particularly well suited, given that it currently acts as the world's largest nongovernmental organization, or relief agency. Kaplan provides examples from numerous areas, and stresses that this is not work for which the United States receives much credit. Finally, he suggests that while one can make the case that the United States should never have gone into Iraq, withdrawing before the job is done would be an even greater mistake.*

I'm going to talk about where I have been because I think you should talk about what you know firsthand, and only what you know recently. To talk about Iraq, or any place, based on a visit three or four years ago is false.

I'm going to focus on the U.S. military in the greater Middle East and its shadow zones. Let me set the stage this way: At any point in time, U.S. Special Operations Command is active in about sixty-seven countries. There is almost no country in the Third World where the U.S. Air Force doesn't have medical teams in any given week. Iraq and Afghanistan are just the tips of the iceberg, literally. The U.S. has almost a thousand troops in Columbia, several hundred in the Philippines. They are all special operations forces on active duty combat. I spent half the summer in sub-Saharan Africa, where U.S. Green Berets were involved in a training program with African countries from Senegal all the way to Ethiopia. Not a line written about any of this stuff in the popular press.

For the most part, the U.S. military conducts bare bones, cheap, effective operations, with little fanfare, where the U.S. taxpayer gets a lot of bang for the buck. Iraq, of course, is the stellar exception to that rule. In the overwhelming majority of these special cases, the U.S. military is not involved in combat at all. It's more involved in humanitarian and disaster relief or training emergency first responders. Whether it's Africa, the Philippines, Columbia, most of Iraq or Afghanistan, the world's greatest nongovernmental organization (NGO) or relief agency is the United States Marines.

In the Asian tsunami, Marines provided about 70 percent of the relief. They had the air assets, the sea assets and it was their fighting experience in Iraq and Afghanistan that allowed them to be the best humanitarian relief workers, because there is very little operational difference between combat and humanitarian relief. It's about quick insertion. It's about access. It's about digging water wells and getting water and electricity started very fast. It's about presence and security patrols. The 19th Special Forces Group, based out of Utah, is now patrolling the streets of New Orleans using the same tactics they did in Afghanistan. The more combat deployments the U.S. military gets, the better relief workers they are, and the more they surge ahead of every other army in the world in that regard. We make a distinction between humanitarian relief and combat, and domestic or foreign deployments. Military people don't do that. Their future is fluid. One deployment merges into the next. The overlapping is incredible.

I spent the first half of the summer in Algeria, embedded with a U.S. Army Special Forces team of twelve Green Berets, one captain, one warrant officer and ten sergeants. It was a typical mission. It was twelve men in a country, to be followed up by another twelve or twenty-four, but one which transformed the state of relations between the U.S. and Algeria. Algeria was the most radical Arab state in the Middle East for many years. It was the head of the nonaligned movement and the father of the "Zionism is Racism" resolution of the mid-1970s. Algeria now is one of the firmest U.S. allies.

Algeria fought in a counterinsurgency against Islamic radicals in the 1990s. Remember reading about Algeria ten years ago? You couldn't ride on a bus. No place was safe. All the Middle East area experts said they couldn't win. The government had to make a compromise. The government did not make a compromise and proved all the area experts wrong. It is now possible to travel around the country in complete security. The Algerian regime basically got mugged by reality, in the form of an Islamic rebellion. Their secret service is one of the reasons why they are providing some of the best intelligence for the U.S. military in Iraq now. The twelve Green Berets I was with were embedded with an Algerian Special Forces company of 150, who had fought heavily against the insurgents in the 1990s. We were on the Mali/Niger border, which is about 1,200 miles south of Algiers. We were there for a month and you could take a shower without a towel, because you dried so fast. If you didn't comb your hair in a second, it frizzed up because of the dryness.

It was a very typical mission for the U.S. military. It's the way things are done around the world, outside of Iraq and Afghanistan. It was small. It was just a small number of force multipliers. The Green Berets there were like other Green Berets and frontline Marine units that I have been with. The ones who are not in Iraq and not in Afghanistan have morale problems precisely because they are not in those countries. The combat arms community, the people who volunteer for frontline commando regiments, are a self-selecting elite. Like any self-selecting elite they want action in their fields. I've only met two types of combat infantry Marines and Green

Berets in the last four years of embedding: those who have been to Iraq and Afghanistan, and those who are pulling every bureaucratic string in order to get deployed there, because it's the best thing since Vietnam, in their opinion. If you join the military, just as you would join the business community as an investor or something, you want to do what you have been trained to do.

Right now U.S.-Algerian relations are on the up and up, but let me go across the region.

Morocco is a big danger. Look at any European terrorist activity and you find Moroccans behind it. Why is that? Morocco has gone through a very messy democratization process over the last ten years, with very difficult demographics and lots of big, poor cities. Morocco is an example of how, while democracy is good in the middle and the long run, in the short run democracy leads to big security problems. When authoritarian systems in South Africa and Russia collapsed, their secret services collapsed, their police forces collapsed and there were new, weak democratic governments—minority governments that provided oxygen systems for criminal networks and terrorists. That's what has happened in Morocco. This may sound very grim and very cynical, but look at it this way: The U.S. military "worst-cased" the scenario for the invasion of Iraq and got the best possible result. It thought about chemical weapons, refugee migrations and everything that could go wrong which, in the end, didn't go wrong. It best-cased the scenario for the occupation and stabilization of Iraq and got the worst possible result. In the world of the military, you always think in worst-case scenarios, because that's what the taxpayer pays you for. And what the U.S. military is thinking about the Middle East right now is the following: that an era of democratization from Morocco to Indonesia means an era of more terrorism for the next ten years, an era of more instability, more Islamic regimes and also an era of more governments who will be less and less able to cope with environmental emergency disasters. After all, it's not just New Orleans. Cairo, too, is on a sea-level floodplain. Most of the Egyptian population lives in the Nile Delta, a very environmentally fragile area. One of the biggest consumers of scholarly studies about environmental fragility is the U.S. military. Books about environmental collapse are all they are reading at Fort Leavenworth.

Let us look at Libya, which has kind of come over and has gone away from radicalism. Already the U.S. military is thinking of training missions there, because you cannot consolidate a country as a stable, moderate country without professionalization of the armed forces. Democratization means military professionalization. One of the hidden hands behind the success of Poland, the Czech Republic, Romania, Bulgaria in the last fifteen years is U.S. military training programs, which got militaries up to snuff and kept them out of trouble by powering them down, training them. It was never NATO, per se. It was basically U.S. military training programs under a NATO umbrella.

I spent a long time in Iraq with the 1st Battalion of the 5th Marine Regiment. I was in the first battle of Fallujah, the first journalist on the scene. I had an extraordinary experience that most people don't get, which was to experience close-quarters urban combat for several days. And I can tell you, I've met presidents, I've briefed prime ministers and I've never been more privileged in my life than to be in the company of the United States Marines. Let me explain why. When fighting starts, when enemy fire emerges, with rocket-propelled grenades (RPGS) mortars, light-medium machine guns, you see eighteen- and nineteen-year-old kids with tattoos all over their bodies suddenly become calculating thirty- and forty-year-olds. I will never forget a light-medium machine gunner on top of a Humvee, a tough kid from the south side of Chicago. He was surrounded, being fired at all over and he did not get off one shot. He did not have a clean shot through his binocs and there were civilians all around. Almost all the fire you heard was indiscriminate fire from the other side. Yet when you're fighting in close-quarters combat, in a very crowded urban environment, there will be a certain number of civilian casualties. The Marine generals warned the Bush administration about this beforehand. In the global media environment we live in, civilian casualties are emphasized by the media, and that exerts political pressure all around. The first battle of Fallujah was the Bush administration at its worst moment in the first term. Nothing happened that was unsurprising. Everything was predictable. You could justify divesting the city. You could justify doing nothing and continuing with surgical strikes. What you could not justify was invading the city and calling off the invasion a week later, because of political pressures that were all predicted and explained to the administration beforehand. That's impulsive behavior. That's unforgivable.

For the most part, in Iraq, in terms of combat active-duty forces, morale has never been better. Self-selecting elites want to be where they have a chance for promotion and to show their skills. According to all studies, 70 to 80 percent of the military voted for Bush in the last election. I would guess about 95 percent of people in the combat arms infantry community did. What the Ivy League professorate is to the Democratic Party, the fighting units of the U.S. military are to the Republicans, and that's statistically provable. Morale is very high.

The problem, the basic structural problem of Iraq, is that the U.S. military, which really means the U.S. Army, is deployed for a mass infantry World War II scenario, with large numbers of troops as a heavy support tail around Baghdad and other major cities, and there are too few fighting units out in the field, where the action is, so to speak. One thing about counterinsurgencies, from the Philippines to Malaysia onward, is that the smaller the number of units and the smaller the size of the actual unit, the more forward it is in a town. If you put five men in a troublesome village and you leave them there for two months to kind of live in the community, make contacts, find out what the community needs, the more you will get out of each troop. But when you send in large numbers of troops just to patrol and then leave at night, you're not really accomplishing anything. What has happened in Iraq is what I call the Westmorlandization of Iraq. The U.S. is fighting Iraq with all the mistakes it made in Vietnam. The U.S. deployed for the Second World War but it's really fighting the nineteenth-century Indian wars against the Apaches and the Sioux, in that sense. That has been the real problem.

The only way to defeat a counterinsurgency cleanly and in a reasonable period of time, in an age of mass global media, is not to have one start in the first place. And so it will be a very, very long, drawn-out war. I don't have an optimistic prediction. But at the same point, let me say I cannot think of anything more irresponsible than pulling out or setting a public timetable for withdrawal. The repercussions would be worse than Vietnam. People said that the domino theory in Southeast Asia was wrong. No, they were wrong. The collapse of Vietnam, within a year or two afterwards, led to millions of people in Ethiopia being enslaved in Stalinist relocation camps. Angola collapsed, as did Nicaragua. The collapse of Vietnam had real repercussions that affected tens of millions of people, particularly in Africa. And the repercussions of Vietnam would be very small compared to those in Iraq; very, very small indeed.

We had an election the other day in Egypt. It was probably the least fixed election in Egyptian history, because of the Internet and the presence of independent bloggers. A friend of mine in the Israeli intelligence told me, "to find out what's going on in Syria these days, check out the independent Syrian bloggers. You get more information from them than you get from the whole Israeli intelligence establishment."

There is a real opening across the Middle East which isn't being sufficiently reported. Tunisia is starting to opening up but we don't hear about it. The report tends to oscillate. For instance, when did the Lebanese Druze tribal chieftain, Walid

Jumblatt, make his comment that Bush may have been right and he was wrong? After the Iraqi elections were seen to be successful and the U.S. was seen to be militarily dominant in the region. And when did the Egyptians decide to hold their least fixed elections in Egyptian history? When did the Syrians decide to open up the Internet? Pin down those dates and you will find those were during news cycles when the U.S. was seen to be strong, seen to be sticking it out. And when the U.S. has bad days in Iraq, then you see retrenchment throughout the region.

One can make a very, very cogent argument that it was the worst mistake for the U.S. to get involved in Iraq in the first place. It's a very reasonable argument. But at the same point, it's also a reasonable argument that, even if it was a great mistake, it would be an even greater mistake to pull out too precipitously now. Consider Afghanistan. The mission there is probably going as best as could be expected, given that during the golden age of governance in Afghanistan, in the 1950s under Zahir Shah, the King only controlled about 50 percent of the country in the first place, the Ring Road and the towns around it. So by Afghans' historical standards, which are the only legitimate standards to use, things have turned out rather well there. And one of the reasons they have is because there has been a relatively small number of U.S. troops in the region (only ten thousand) and most of them are never seen by Afghans because they are out in the war zones along the Pakistan-Afghan border and in southern Afghanistan. What Afghans see in the cities is the heavily international North Atlantic Treaty Organization (NATO) force. There is very little anti-Americanism in Afghanistan, because they don't see that many Americans in the first place. The deployment in Afghanistan is very right. It's been very, very wrong in Iraq.

If I was going to make a prediction, I would say that the next big place where U.S. Army special forces may be deployed, over the next five or eight years, is the tribal agencies of Pakistan. Urdu is a coming exotic language in the U.S. defense establishment. We are entering a world where we have increasingly large concentrated numbers of human beings in more and more absolute numbers living in environmentally fragile zones than ever before in history. Two-thirds of the Chinese population lives in flood zones. This is going to lead to all kinds of disasters. Political stresses are going to lead to this and that. What we are seeing right now is the militarization of humanitarian relief aid. Nothing happened in New Orleans until troops landed. There are all of these figures from aid agencies about how they are active in thirty or forty African countries. When you get to these countries, there are Peace Corps workers, nongovernmental organizations active in the capital and the environs. The rest of the country is usually only accessible for aid purposes to one Western military or another to provide the aid. Increasingly, where you need water wells dug, where you need food brought, where systems of society have broken down, there are also places where you have insurgencies, and therefore it's unsafe for civilians to go in. The United Nations Office for the Coordinations of Human Affairs (OCHA) is just the beginning of this new world. A more democratic Middle East means a more tumultuous, unstable Middle East, if only for the first ten years. More democracy in the middle and the long run is going to lead to more disasters and more upheavals. Therefore the more militaries that are deployed, Canadian or American or whatever, the better they are going to get at relief aid, because there isn't that much difference operationally between combat and providing disaster relief.

———

Q: You predicted ten more years of terrorism, ten more years of counterinsurgency, ten more years of humanitarian relief efforts in half a dozen countries, maybe a dozen across the Middle East. On the other hand, you said that there are only eight thousand Green Berets to do this job. How do you combine those two facts, and can other countries help and, if so, how?

A: Let me deal with Iran first. Iran is not a regime. It's a system with different power centers and because it's a system, it cannot be overthrown. Iraq was one man, but Iran has different levels of power all competing with each other. You have the goons in the security services and the radical ayatollahs. You have former presidents. Then you have technocrats in the Cabinet. The result is that it becomes impossible for any of them to make any really new direction in foreign policy because they get sniped at by the other two or three.

We look at Iran as very sinister but it's actually a very undynamic regime. There can be no Nixon to China in Iran because when Nixon went to China he only had to deal with a few people. It was very much nineteenth-century court diplomacy. But in Iran, you're dealing with dozens upon dozens of people that you have to convince to change in a particular direction. I would say that even the moderate pro-Westerners in Iran want a nuclear option.

Once Iran gets a nuclear capability, even if, for the sake of argument, there was a change in regime and more moderate leaders took over, those new moderate leaders would never give up the nuclear option because of this tremendous sense of Persian nationalism, which supersedes Islamism in Iran. Remember, Persia was the world's first superpower. All you have to do is read Herodotus and the ancient Greek writers to see this. Historic status has real, actual meaning to Persians in Tehran today. They see themselves as a superpower in the region.

When I wrote *The Ends of the Earth* in the early mid-90s, I thought there would be a change in Iran. If you were a man from Mars and went backpacking around Iran, it was one of the most pro-American places in the world because the Iranians had already gone through an Islamic revolution. They were in a post-cynical phase and they associated an Islamic revolution with destruction of the middle class. On the other hand, when you traveled through Egypt, which was a pro-American ally, all you heard was anti-Americanism everywhere.

The Iranian regime has real legs. It is going to be around for a long time, and unlike the late 1970s, there is no sense of counterrevolution. The revolutionaries in the 1970s thought they were bringing about Utopia and they got a regime as worse, or worse, than the Shah. In terms of Green Berets, there are eight thousand of them around the world divided into five groups all with area specialties, but the Marines are training more and more area specialists in unconventional war, which sounds sinister but it really means using a lot of techniques, including humanitarian relief, to turn populations to your side.

Remember, what I've been describing is the situation out-side Iraq and Afghanistan, where the U.S. military paradigm is to use ten or twelve men, or a hundred at the most, to become a hinge in changing relations with a country. Generally, it tends to work. Remember, everybody hates imperialism, but when the U.S. acts in a classic imperialist manner, like training a pan-African intervention force for future Darfurs, which is what is happening in sub-Saharan Africa right now, people like that. Iraq is a perversion of classic imperialism, rather than an accurate expression of it.

Q: You speak of the militarization of humanitarian aid as if it's a reality out there on the ground and this is certainly something that has come to alarm those who have been doing humanitarian aid for many years. Organizations like Médecins Sans Frontières have, of late, deplored the fact that they are confused with military operations, that they are regarded with suspicion, that they are more likely to be tar-geted for kidnapping or obstruction when it comes to their work. What would you say is the downside to the way the United States is militarizing humanitarian aid?

A: If it's effective in helping the people under stress, there is no downside. If you're a Bolivian peasant in southern Bolivia, where the U.S. Air Force has been inoculating cattle and other livestock against diseases as a form of humanitarian aid, you don't care if the people helping you are wearing uniforms or not. All you care about is the efficiency and the quality of the help. The aim of humanitarian aid is not to protect those giving aid, but to help the victims. The reality is that militaries are more able to take risks to themselves than are civilian workers. I'm not just talking about American militarization of humanitarian aid. I'm talking about other Western militaries as well, like the French in West Africa. Or take the case of Niger. Eighty percent of the country is inaccessible to Western relief organizations. The only way to get relief there is through cooperation with the Nigerian military, which is what France, the U.S. and others have done. To me there is only one criterion for aid: the efficiency and speed in which it helps those under duress. And if that's better done by militaries, then so be it.

Q: What do you believe is the long-term sustainability of the policy of humanitarian intervention in the United States, a country where you have apparently not recently been embedded? Are the Democrats, if elected, likely to reverse these intelligent policies you've been describing?

A: I don't think the Democrats would have performed any better over the past few years, except the problems might have been different. The problems in New Orleans have a deeper significance which relates to the fact that we are going to have increasingly complex, large urban concentrations in environmentally fragile zones. This includes the whole coast of Florida and parts of the West Coast. What happened in New Orleans was that there wasn't sufficient investment in infrastructure in the years and decades prior to Hurricane Katrina.

What I'm deeply worried about is not the military. It's that we're facing a world and challenges—inside the U.S. perhaps, inside China and India for sure—where it's unclear if democracy with four-year election cycles can handle these problems. If you go to the deeper roots of why there wasn't the necessary investment in infrastructure, it's because there is no political payoff for politicians who are always running for reelection of one sort or another.

China has opened up its economy, but it has not opened up its political system because it feels that the way to manage these environmental stresses is precisely by not opening its political system. It's unclear that India can handle the environmental situation, particularly if you look at the future demographics of Delhi and other places. I think we have to take a real hard look at the viability of democracies in complex, environmentally stressed societies on constant election cycles.

Q: What's the alternative? China is not an example for dealing with issues like pandemics—look at the problem they created for themselves with respect to the SARS issue. The Communist Party put the lid on the damn thing and if there hadn't been a few individuals capable of getting the word out, we would have had an absolute mess. That has nothing to do with electoral cycles. It has to do with a regime that simply doesn't want to report bad news to the population.

A: I think the great intellectual conceit is to think that there's a clean solution to every problem. I don't believe there is a clean solution to this. One of the constants of ancient Greek and Roman literature, which was carried out by the founding fathers, Madison and Hamilton, when they talked about wanting a republic (not a democracy), is that they always envisioned a mixed regime that had elements of democracy and elements of authoritarianism. The authoritarian elements were only having elections periodically and only giving people a chance every few years to replace or judge their electors.

What they never envisioned was the world of constant public opinion polls, constant overbearing media klieg-light scrutiny that we have today because of the development of technology. So democracy itself is facing stresses that it has never faced before. The examples of the Soviet Union and China are extreme examples of authoritarian systems. I'm saying that the kind of system we have in Western democracies may not be up to the environmental challenges, but that's saying something totally different than justifying the systems in the Soviet Union and China.

Q: The parallels you drew between Iraq and the Vietnam experience were quite interesting. You made the point that this is the best the military has had it since Vietnam. Does being embedded with the troops pose a risk to your point of view as a journalist and specifically to your objectivity as a journalist? Do you run the risk of seeing things perhaps solely through the soldiers' own human-interest stories, perhaps romanticizing what they're going through; and, if so, how do you counter that?

A: I think that even at the height of embedding, the media has a far more incestuous relationship with politicians, academics, the relief community and businesspeople than it has with any branch of the military. And what unites all these other subcultures is that they're all in a high-income-level strata. Even relief workers tend to be young people who are often from well-off families looking for adventure of one sort or another. The military is different because the military tends to come from the working classes. Not the poor but the lower-middle working classes. Therefore I find a lot of criticism of embedding to be a form of class prejudice. Embedding now offers the only opportunity for upper income elites to have a sustained meaningful relationship with members of the working class from their own country.

Q: How do you avoid being co-opted when you are embedded, not politically but psychologically? There is a famous phrase by Samuel Johnson, "Every man feels meanly of himself who has never been a soldier." You are a talker and analyzer. The people you are with are not good with words. They do things. And there's nothing that a person who's good at words is more respectful of than a man who can do something with his hands. You know, fix a car, be a carpenter. That seems to me to be your real problem as an embedded person. Am I right?

A: That's a beautiful way of putting it. And on a recent sailing vacation, I read Dr. Johnson's *Journey to the Hebrides*, so I'm very familiar with that quotation. You're totally right.

Here's how I would put it: I'm a magazine writer and an author. I'm not a daily news journalist, writing eight-hundred-word news stories. My job is to kind of get into a subculture, to get inside it, live it, accept it like a nineteenth-century travel writer and let that subculture communicate with the public directly. Since these people don't have a voice, I will give them a voice.

While I was in Fallujah in April 2004, I had a Canadian colleague, Patrick Graham, embedded a few hundred yards away from me. He was with the insurgents and he wrote a piece for *Harper's*. I wrote my piece for the *Atlantic Monthly*. My piece had tremendous sympathy for the Marines. His had a lot of understanding for the insurgents. When the two of us got together afterwards, we didn't have a fight or an argument or anything like that. We had a great, long chat because we were both doing something useful. There's a whole realm of journalism where you just concentrate on where you are and show that reality with as much texture and minutiae as you possibly can. That is what I was doing. That is what Patrick was doing. An intelligent reader will read two different pieces and will be able to get a much more complex reality out of it.

Q: What work have you done as an embedded journalist with a working class other than the Marines?

A: I was embedded with the U.S. Army Special Forces in Columbia, the Philippines, Afghanistan, Djibouti, Niger and Algeria. I've been embedded with the U.S. Air Force in various Pacific islands. I spent a month on a fast-attack nuclear submarine just two months ago, the USS *Houston*. I spent a month on the USS *Penfold*, a guided missile destroyer, watching its humanitarian relief operations a few miles off the coast of Indonesia before sailing back with it to Honolulu. It was a great experience to sail on a surface ship across the whole Pacific and get out in the morning and see the big waves and the ocean. I expect to do more embedding with the Navy Seals and the Air Force on some of its newer missions, which are on-the-ground tactical things, such as laying dirt-strip runways in Third World countries, in order to have quick insertion and really fast access.

Q: The most powerful justification that the Bush administration has for its intervention in Iraq is an argument for the democratization of a Middle East that has been plagued with authoritarian regimes for fifty years. Yet your argument is, in effect, one for enlightened authoritarianism. There are no enlightened authoritarian regimes in that part of the world. From what we know, from people like Amartya Sen and others, the governments that do worst at handling environmental catastrophes are undemocratic governments that have no social contract with their local populations. They do worse at handling floods and famines, and many of the regimes in the Middle East have an absolutely horrific record precisely on this score.

A: First of all, I disagree with Amartya Sen because, in his research, he takes the most extreme authoritarian regimes,

THE AMERICAN MILITARY AS NGO

particularly Ethiopia under Mengistu Haile Mariam, as his examples. Let's go across the Middle East. Let's start with King Hassan in Morocco and his son, King Mohammed the Sixth. This is an enlightened, quasi-mixed, semi-authoritarian regime. The Algerian regime was just legitimized by free and fair elections, but still rules in an authoritarian manner. President Zine El Abidine Ben Ali of Tunisia increased the middle class from 5 percent to 60 percent with no oil wealth whatsoever, under very mild authoritarianism. President Ali Abdullah Saleh of Yemen, again a kind of quasi-authoritarian dictator who holds free and fair democratic elections, has a parliament that snipes at him all the time and he tolerates it. King Hussein of Jordan, the late King Hussein of Jordan, King Abdullah—they listen to a parliament that is freely elected when they want but, on key national security issues, they abrogate the decision of the parliament. If you play this game of looking at the worst regimes and seeing how they react to disasters, you can come up with any thesis you want. But if you look at what I call gray-area regimes, which tend to dominate the region heavily, you'll come up with a very different reality.

Fouad Ajami and Bernard Lewis give very elegant defenses of democratization in the Middle East, which basically I support. But if you talk to them, they'll also say that in the short-run there will be tremendous security problems.

Today, I have pointed out the tactical short-term problems by talking about what I have seen in the last year or two. I've been with many militaries, whether it's the U.S., the

Canadian, the Australian or the Japanese military, who are forced by their mandate with the taxpayer to only think in worst-case scenarios.

Q: Is it fair to apply the model of Morocco to Iraq since the latter is a rich oil-producing country? If oil production can be brought up to optimal levels and the wealth can be spread around, can't we avoid the problems that you've described in Morocco as attached to the overpopulated poor cities? Furthermore, isn't Iraq really a situation where the flypaper strategy is working and where the Americans and their allies are attracting terrorists or inspiring terrorists from all over the Muslim world to Iraq? Prior to the London bombings in July, for nearly a year there had been almost no serious instance outside Iraq, Afghanistan and Israel. We must be killing large numbers of these people or otherwise neutralizing them, while every week training more Iraqis to take this over for themselves on behalf of a government that is acquiring some legitimacy.

A: The per capita wounded in action and killed in action of American troops in Iraq is much, much lower than in Vietnam. It's the safest war the Americans have fought, the safest hot war.

Patience and persistence always win and others have made strong arguments about the progress we're making. Here's the problem. To win a counterinsurgency in an age of global media is very, very tough because even if you have deaths that are not tactically or strategically significant, they demoralize the home front because of the relationship between the media and the public. I think withdrawing or setting a timetable for withdrawal is absolutely the most irresponsible thing that anyone can do and I think it will backfire on the Democrats if they go in that direction. It's unclear that they will.

And yes, you can get the oil production started but the problem the U.S. has had all along is, as one Iraqi resident said to me, the Marines went in to look at this sprawling Shiite town of 85,000 and people were screaming at the Marines, "How come we don't have running water or electricity? The democratic town council you set up are a bunch of thieves," and on and on they went. If you're an average Iraqi, you look at the Americans and you say, "These people toppled a dictator we never thought could be toppled, and yet they can't get the water and the electricity started."

Even if you have all the oil going it is still going to be an enormous infrastructure challenge to provide these services, because it's only at the level of running water and electricity that oil stops being abstract and becomes substantive to the average Iraqi on the ground. If you listen in at these town council meetings, you hear these problems: "Why isn't the water running?" or "Why isn't the electricity going?" or "The pipes have collapsed. People are siphoning off the electricity. The contractor who came in to put in a bid for new pipes was killed because he wasn't from this town." It's a whole array of problems that Saddam was able to manage with sheer brutality and authoritarianism and the U.S. can't because the military doesn't operate that way.

So even with the oil running, it's going to be a real challenge to make that palpable to the average Iraqi. Only when the average person sees progress in terms of less crime and running water will you have more and more snitches providing you with information against insurgents, which is the real tipping point in this.

TRADING STABILITY FOR PROGRESS

CHRISTOPHER HITCHENS
NOVEMBER 17, 2005

Prolific and iconoclastic journalist Christopher Hitchens has long been on record as a supporter of the U.S.-led intervention in Iraq. Here, he seeks to explain his stance, arguing that those who claim the recent incursion into the region interrupted fifty years of peace are wearing blinders. Stressing that the Iran-Iraq War, the burning of the Kuwaiti oil fields and the destruction of the Marsh Arabs cannot reasonably be called acts of peace, Hitchens reminds his listeners of the progress that has been made. Arguing that events in the Middle East now are following a similar path to those in Europe twenty or twenty-five years ago, Hitchens vows to continue supporting the Iraqi patriots, whether they are winning, losing or mired in a long struggle.

One of the things that marks for me the regime change that I've come to defend in Iraq, and want to advance, is the thought that an embassy in Canada that was once run by psychopathic taxi drivers and people who sheltered terrorists and gave out bribes to local politicians, and engaged in smuggling of all kinds of awful materials, and who were the envoys of a psychopathic hereditary crime family, should now be occupied by an honorable man in Ottawa, Howar Ziad, a very old comrade of mine. Ziad is a man who was a *real* insurgent; a member of an actual people's army in Iraq: the Kurdish Peshmerga who were fighting against Saddam Hussein's regime when we were not, and a man of wide learning and culture. It's in the details, I sometimes feel, that one can sense what change really means.

Before I press on with that, I'd be untrue to myself, I'd like to think, if I didn't disagree with my friend David Frum's very generous introduction just for a second. It would be quite false to compare me to George Orwell and I've certainly never sought the comparison. George Orwell never had a steady job, was always ill, was often censored, took a bullet through the throat in Spain just down the front line, I think, from the Mackenzie-Papineau brigade. Heroism of that kind has never been required remotely of me. I blush to think how risk-free my life is compared to people like Ambassador Ziad and others.

But to resume, I was once asked why I wanted to become a journalist and I found that I replied so that I wouldn't have to rely on the press for information. And to know people like Ambassador Ziad. Another example? To go recently to Blair House in Washington to meet President Jalal Talabani, the first elected president of Iraq; to have recently, with David and his wife Danielle, a large number of Iraqi and Kurdish democrats in my home, including the man who led the guerrilla warfare in the southern marshes against Saddam Hussein for eighteen years. To be with these people is to feel very humble and very modest and also, in my case, very angry.

Because when I read the *New York Times* the following day or the *Washington Post* or, indeed, some of the Canadian press, too, it's as if these meetings were never taking place. It's as if these people did not exist. It's as if Iraq, now retaken by its own people—who are engaged in a discussion about a constitution with regular votes and elections, and a parliament, and six television channels and twenty-one newspapers—was under occupation by its citizens.

Going to Iraq is like watching a fire burning under water. One sees these arguments going on, these passionate engagements and differences and disagreements and talks about the future, and remembers that three years ago it would have been death to possess a satellite dish. It would have been death not just for you, but for your family. And the death would not have been an easy one. To remember at that time the marshes—the oldest ecology in the Middle East, the largest wetlands in the region, home to a civilization that's remembered from Biblical times—were drained and then dried out and then burned out by Saddam Hussein to destroy a people he didn't like.

And the fire from that atrocity—considered by UNESCO to be the greatest environmental crime ever committed—the fire was so intense and so filthy that it could be seen from the space shuttle *Mercury*.

That's what was going on. And the people of Kurdistan were living in villages and towns that had been ethnically cleansed to the tune of, perhaps, three-quarters of a million people dead and poisoned with chemical weapons, the injuries of which are still burning. They still hurt. They still burn. And whose children were unable to breathe, were crippled and ruined by nerve weapons and by gas. To see this transition is, to me, an absolutely remarkable and essential thing.

The question that's somewhere in the back of everyone's mind must be this: Is this the beginning of something or is it just the end of a terrible period when the United States and the international community couldn't make up their minds on how to resolve twenty, thirty years of failed statecraft in the region? Is this the product of our wrong policies? Is it the terminus of some very bad administrations? Is it the responsibility we've incurred from our indifference and our callousness about the region? Or is it the beginning of a new epoch? Or could it possibly be both? I want to give two or three examples, if I may.

You will all have been following the report by United Nations envoy Detlev Mehlis about the state of affairs in Syria, where the Baath Party regime, not unlike its former counterpart in Baghdad, is based on an ethnic minority and a confessional minority. This party has ruled by divide-and-rule policies and by military and police tactics for two generations now, and appears to be in the process of implosion because of its policy of death squad and mobster rule in Lebanon.

This is precipitated by two things. First, something that I hope all of you find encouraging: a mass movement among Lebanese of all confessions—Sunni, Shiite, Maronite, Christian, Greek Orthodox and Druze—to recover the sovereignty of their country after nearly twenty years of ignominious occupation and extraordinary corruption and cruelty. And to do so, really, without a shot being fired. It was their civil society simply folding their arms and expressing defiance which caused the Syrian army to grudgingly withdraw and then to resume its campaign of assassination and intimidation from across the border. Is this plus or is it minus? Is this positive or is this negatively charged?

We have on the one side an extraordinary affirmation among the Lebanese, which we think may soon be emulated among the Syrians. And on the other, the threat of disorder, of revenge, of further confessional dislikes and rivalries which could be not just deleterious in themselves, but to the region as a whole.

I want you very earnestly to consider whether that's positive or negative. I also want you to remember the words of Walid Jumblatt, an acquaintance of mine, the leader of the Lebanese Socialist Party and the great leader of the Lebanese Druze community, who says openly, as a frequent critic of

American foreign policy, that he doesn't believe this moment could ever have arrived in Lebanon if the keystone state of autocracy and tyranny in the region—the Baathist state of Saddam Hussein—if that keystone had not been knocked out by the coalition intervention. He believes it is that that has inaugurated this Lebanese renaissance. Am I willing to take his word for it? No. I'm not willing to take anybody's word for it. Rather, I should say that it's an impressive testimony of evidence against interest and that it has, up to now, been very often Dr. Jumblatt's role to be the leading critic of American policy in the region. In other words, it's testimony from an impressive quarter.

I'll give you a second example. Dr. Saad Eddin Ibrahim, the heroic Egyptian academic and social scientist who decided to take the government at its word a few years ago and say, "All right. It is all right to do social research. It's all right to ask people what they really think out in the countryside about the government and the system. It's okay to take opinion polls. When we have pretend elections, it's all right to send poll watchers and election monitors and even to invite them from outside, just to act as if we did have a democracy in Egypt and maybe the more we pretend to have one the nearer we'd get to actually getting one." He was rewarded for this with a long period of solitary confinement, which led to an international campaign which was successful ultimately. Since his release, he is toasted from one end of Egypt to the other as an unimpeachable man, as the model of the independent intellectual and the brave human soul.

Well, I had a long discussion with him at a conference of Arab democrats in the state of—actually Kingdom of—Qatar a few months ago. He said to me, "Look, without the intervention in Iraq, the logjam would never have been broken. The tundra would never have unfrozen. The wall would never have come down." He was completely persuaded, obviously. In fact, he made an analogy that gave me some pause.

How many of you here tonight went to a Trafalgar Day celebration last month? Less than I thought. Or perhaps more than I would have liked because, as someone born in Portsmouth and into a long line of officers in the Royal Navy, I've always had a soft spot for Admiral Nelson and, indeed, for Trafalgar Day. But I can never celebrate it as much as I'd like because I'm not sure I can ever forgive Nelson for defeating Napoleon Bonaparte's expedition to Egypt in 1798. That expedition discovered, for us, the Rosetta Stone and unlocked the key of the hieroglyphic; but that very expedition was planned as a rationalist French intervention in the region. I know it sounds odd, but there you have it.

They brought scientists and republican political theorists and great teachers and men of medicine and learning to Egypt and began what was acknowledged by all Egyptians at the time as a great renaissance, a great new encounter with the West, an unfreezing, undoing of the millennial torpor that had covered over the country for so long.

I sometimes wish that Nelson hadn't sunk Bonaparte's fleet at Aboukir Bay and that he hadn't had to sail home, because that period is still looked upon by many Arab modernists and democrats as a great moment of potential opportunity, perhaps the one that they missed. Many of them now talk as if history has happened again from the outside, which they resent in some ways. It's an insult to their pride. But nonetheless, from outside has come a dynamic force; an influence that once exerted, once implanted, can't be unimplanted, can't be undone. Remember those six new television stations in Baghdad. Remember the twenty-one new newspapers in Iraq. Many people are trying to blow them up as we speak, but the audience they've created, the difference that they've made, is beyond our calculation.

We won't know for many years what forces have been unleashed in the Arab mind, in the Middle Eastern mind, but I think we have some grounds for optimism on that score. And there's another aspect of it that interests me. The people I mentioned, Ambassador Ziad, President Talabani of Iraq, Walid Jumblatt of the Lebanese socialist Party, Saad Eddin Ibrahim of what we might call the Egyptian civil society movement—all of these men have been known to me for some time. They all used to be fairly red politically.

At a reception for President Talabani in Blair House a few weeks ago, the one I mentioned to you, we all looked around, these Arabs and Kurds and their few friends who had come, and said, "We wonder if George Bush knows how many ex-Marxists he has staying with him tonight." "Probably not, was the view."

President Talabani told me that every time he quarreled with Paul Bremer—the envoy of Kissinger Associates, who was the viceroy of Bush in Iraq for a while—every time they quarreled, Bremer would dismiss him saying, "No, no. That's just your old Marxism coming out, Jalal."

Now, it's of interest to me that what used to be the Middle Eastern, Marxist left has moved now to taking a civil society stand that is not just subjectively but objectively, as it were, pro-American. The Iraqi Communist Party—a great civil society force in itself under Saddam—joined the provisional government in Iraq on the first day. Kanan Makiya, whom I would describe as the Dubcek or the Solzhenitsyn of the Iraqi dissident movement, wrote, in exile, the great anatomy of the regime that everyone had to read, *The Republic of Fear*, and its successor, *Cruelty and Silence*. This was the great unpicking of the relationship between Baathism, Stalinism and fascism. Kanan Makiya has been known to me for many years as probably one of the very few Trotskyites left alive who deserves the name "Intellectual." He is a man of extraordinary physical and moral and intellectual courage.

Now, that's interesting to me because it replicates what was happening in Eastern Europe about twenty to twenty-five years ago, when a large proportion of the old left intelligentsia began to realize that the system of the Warsaw Pact and of "Comecon" Soviet domination of state planning could not go on, could not go on in the old way; that they needed to reapply themselves to the ideas of pluralism, free trade and the free movement of people and ideas.

At the time, people thought, "No, it will never happen. The Russian glacier will never melt. The Berlin Wall will never fall. There may be changes. There may be rebellions, but it's a permanent geographical fact." That's what the realists all believed. That's why Henry Kissinger wouldn't have

Aleksandr Solzhenitsyn invited to the White House and told President Ford to keep him waiting outside.

I would very much welcome a challenge on this point, but it seems to me when a convergence and realignment of this kind is happening, it may be a premonitory signal that the most benighted region, the region that has been sunk in the most oppression, the most ignorance, the most backwardness and the most cruelty, may not be immune to the force that swept the Philippines in the early '80s. That "people power" led to—and culminated in—the wonderful Velvet Revolution of 1989 in Europe. Its example has been so useful to us since in the Ukraine and in many other countries that had been, it was thought, in some way *in partibus infidelium*; not good enough to share in our pluralism and our free markets and our free inquiry.

And, of course, I'm quite wrong in forgetting to include the extraordinary moment in Tiananmen Square in early 1989. Now, I've just given you the way in which I think the glass is a bit better than half full. But returning to my original question, some people look at these heartening and, in fact, inspiring developments and they don't see progress. They don't see the hope of change. They don't see liberation. They see only one thing.

They see instability. We were used to President Assad. You knew where you stood with him. We understood Syria then. Now what? What's going to happen if he goes? The querulous voice of the natural conservative, the one who fears change. Now my response to this, which is a very strongly entrenched opinion in Washington and getting more so, is twofold. First, these regimes could not go on in the old way. They were declining of their own nature. They were falling of their own weight. We did not start the violence in Syria and Lebanon. The regime began to sponsor terror and violence. It's destabilizing itself. How stable therefore was that, even if you left the question of justice to one side?

But increasingly in the nation's capital, my nation's capital that is to say, you hear the voices of those who say, "Regime change is imprudent. What happens if the Saudi Arabian government is challenged? How will we know who's boss? How will we know what proxies we should be ruling through? How will the CIA know which bit of the military to use for its next coup? How will it know which democrat to assassinate? It's cruel to leave the CIA guessing in this way."

The $44-billion budget, as we've just been told in another leak, the agency that couldn't get a single American inside the Taliban or Al Qaeda, whereas Mr. John Walker Lindh of Marin County was able to join it, unsubsidized—this is the agency that reported that Saddam Hussein neither could nor would invade Kuwait. An unbroken record of failure as well as of crime and subversion, yet these voices are now being listened to and replayed through our media as if they were the more statesmanlike, the more cautious, the more prudent, the more—I'll say it again—realistic.

The apotheosis of this mentality was to be found in a recent essay in the *New Yorker* by my friend, Jeffrey Goldberg, profiling General Brent Scowcroft who, with George Bush, Sr., wrote the book on why to leave Saddam Hussein alone in

1991 and who has ever since hewed to the view that Iraq was better off with than without Saddam Hussein. General Scowcroft also regards the developments in Syria with a very jaundiced eye, and Lebanon, too, and says that he's already beginning to feel nervous because, he said, it might be the end. And I'm quoting here directly from one of our leading national security officers and intellectuals. "Because it might be the end," he says, "of fifty years of peace."

Now, I only sketched in some of the things that have happened in the last fifty years or twenty-five years in the Middle East. Would anyone here be bold enough to put up their hand and say that was a period of peace? I would think not.

I would say the ignition of the Kuwaiti oil fields by Saddam Hussein, the deaths of a million and a half people in the Iran-Iraq War, which was provoked by Jimmy Carter's promiscuity in allowing—indeed encouraging—Saddam Hussein to attack Iran; the genocide in Kurdistan, the planned destruction of an entire people and the erasure of its culture taking place in our full view in northern Iraq; these don't deserve to be called episodes in a period of peace. So I'm afraid that's why I must indict the realist mentality, first for its cynicism, in other words, and second for its naiveté. I think the two things go very well together.

My friend Martin Amis once said of somebody that he had no sense of humor. He added, "And by saying that, I really mean to impugn his seriousness." Often the most naive are the most cynical. They believe themselves to be hard-boiled. In fact, they're very soggy. They make very unreliable moral and political guides.

So I'll have to say for myself, and I had probably better do this in closing, that I've taken my side with these comrades in Iraq, and in Kurdistan, and in Egypt, and in Lebanon and in Syria, and I'm going to be with them win or lose.

I'm on their side whether they're victorious or whether they're being defeated or whether they're mired in a long struggle. I've picked my turf here. I don't mean to try and recruit any of you to it, but I would hope that if you want to challenge me you will also take me up on my implied challenge to the realists, which is to consider the horrors of peace.

TRADING STABILITY FOR PROGRESS

Q: What is Iran going to look like five to ten years from now?

A: Iran, of all of the examples I could have mentioned, is in a way the most hopeful and also the most sobering. I describe it in my essay as an "as if" society. It votes as if it had real elections. They actually produce candidates as if there really were candidates, and people vote as if they really were electors, and then they pretend to count the votes and they do everything except actually have an election, because everyone's screened out who could possibly be a nuisance beforehand. They act as if they had a free press; they publish different newspapers and different opinions, within a certain circumscribed limit. Most people actually get their news, however, from satellite dishes, from cell phones, from the very large and very important and very democratic Iranian diaspora that is very extensive in Canada as well as in the U.S. and Europe.

What has happened in Iran is partly due to demographics. In the insane war that they've prolonged for so long after the defeat of Saddam Hussein's forces in Iraq and trying to conquer Iraq, the Iranians threw away three-quarters of a million or so of their young, and many others were hopelessly mutilated and disabled. These are First World War–type figures. There's a huge hospital in Tehran that deals with nothing but lung cases from poison gas. It's the sort of stuff Canadians could come back from Vimy and tell you about. It's that kind of a war.

With this tremendous birth dearth, the mullahs had no choice but to finance a program for Iranian women to have more babies and to subsidize large families. These programs worked and they're now faced with a baby boomerang. In other words, there's this extraordinarily young generation, probably half the population of Iran is under twenty-five, all of whom wish they lived in Marin County, although it depends which ones you ask. But all of whom basically wish they lived in Western Europe, or Canada or the United States and whose models as to fashion and music and dress and literature are very much of that type. In the long run, therefore, the society will simply outgrow the regime. Within Iran, there is a society that is outgrowing the state. We have to do everything we can to encourage that outcome and watch it with real admiration and solidarity, and I think we will live to see very great things in Iran. It's not in nature that the civilization of Persia and a people as polished and sophisticated and various and versatile as that should be kept in childhood and servitude by a bunch of verminous clerics. It won't last.

I want it to last a little bit longer because I would like to see the complete discredit of Islamic rule. We don't have to run the experiment anew every time for every society, but if you do try and run a society out of the Quran, this is what will happen to you. You will go bankrupt. Your people will be illiterate. There will be untreated disease and misery, and everyone will want to leave, and there will be cultural stultification on a terrible order. Let's see how the whole experiment goes and then get rid of them, and let's help the Iranian people to do so.

Q: As part of the elite former Marxist group now embracing a commitment to a model of democracy, how do you diagnose the liberal left of Europe and North America's increasing disregard for the logical merits of democracy and its actual moral value as an imperative?

A: I never said there was a Marxist elite, comrade, but I know what you mean when you inquire about leftist pessimism. I began to notice around the time of the war in Bosnia Herzegovina that the left, in general, had become a status quo force, a conservative force. In other words, it for the most part argued to stay out of Bosnia—"Yugoslavia is too complicated to be bothering with." "It's dangerous." "It's unstable." "It's best left alone"—ignoring the fact that the recrudescence of ethnic fascism on the borders of southern Europe is something that could easily have spread to Hungary and Romania. "No, no. It's too risky. It might even lead to casualties." For the left to become a status quo force was a historically very important thing. I deplored it and then I began to deplore it more in advance because I thought conservatism of that kind doesn't just stay conservative. It will become reactionary and that's what has happened since.

There are people, quite a lot of them, who look at the forces of bin Ladenism and jihadism and they say, "Well, it's not perfect, perhaps. It has its drawbacks, but any movement against globalization is better than none. This will do till a better movement comes along." I've heard it said. I hear it all the time. They regard these people as a protest against unemployment and poverty and backwardness whereas, of course, they are the cause of it. They are the cause of misery. Their bombs in Jordan and Indonesia reduced the national income by several points and made the difference between many millions of Jordanians and Indonesians making minimum wage or not. They produce unemployment and want and degradation. They don't deserve the credit for protesting against it. That's what they've created.

Q: This question has to do with who intelligent people, if not the intelligentsia per se, are speaking for? What about all those people in Iraq who are not "intelligent"? We can have a great lot of ideas for them but will they go with it and how will they go with it? Are you not biased toward an intelligentsia view of things?

A: It's very plain to me that even some of the mainstream liberal left regards George W. Bush as more of a threat than, say, Saddam Hussein. This is absurd. This is the reduction of moral equivalence to moral idiocy and deserves to be called by its right name. But, above all, it's extremely reactionary in all its aspects, which is why I stressed more what you might call the Iraqi intelligentsia. Maybe I spend more of my time with Iraqis of that sort but I promise you, if you talk to Abu Hatim—the present leader who led the resistance in the marshes to Saddam Hussein and liberated most of that part of Iraq without American or British help—or to the Kurdish Peshmerga or many of the foot soldiers who run the new Iran and are trying to drag it out of the ruins and the wreckage, you would be impressed by their plebian and proletarian staunchness just as much as you can be impressed by the intellectual character of the elite.

It's not the act of an ivory tower, pointy-headed person to stand in line in the hot sun to wait to cast the first vote of your life and bring your family along, when you've been plausibly told that you can be killed for doing that or for trying it. For the people of Iraq to have done that twice already, and for a third time next month, when they know that the polling places are targets for suicide murderers and so on, is something that I wish more intellectuals had the courage to do.

Q: In Canada, we have difficulty in seeing that the largely unilateral and overwhelming application of force by the United States was the best way of countering the regime of Saddam Hussein. Is this some sort of lesson for the future?

A: I always try to be polite when the word unilateral is mentioned and I never succeed. If the intervention in Iraq in March of 2003 had not occurred, it would have fallen to Saddam Hussein in May of 2003 to appoint the chair of the United Nations Special Committee on Disarmament. That's the fact of the matter. Just as it fell to Colonel Gaddafi to appoint the vice-chair of the UN Special Committee on Human Rights. I think one has to realize the point at which an institution has become self-satirizing and beyond absurd. The United States–British initiative at the United Nations was as follows: there was a thesaurus of resolutions regarding not just weapons of mass destruction but support for terrorism, refusal to account for the missing persons in Kuwait or to make compensation to Kuwait, for a whole host of things. These resolutions, which were passed unanimously in some cases, were not enforced. The idea then was to cut with the grain of the spirit of the UN, as expressed with the letter and the spirit of the resolutions.

What is more unilateral, to do that or to say, as the government of Mr. Chirac said, that we will veto this initiative under any circumstances? Now, I'll be happy on the day that the *New York Times* considers French policy as the unilateralist, simple-minded, selfish, sectarian provincial colonialism that it is. But it never does. France detonates weapons of mass destruction in the atmosphere in the Pacific and shoots people who protest against it without even consulting the United Nations or the local authorities and states, which sends troops to support the government in Rwanda, which bombards the government and people of Ivory Coast, without even telling the United Nations, without being asked.

The term unilateralist is reserved only for one state. Now, put the opposite case. Imagine that we had not had to undergo the shame of watching what happened in Rwanda as spectators. In fact, we were such spectators that we were more or less complicit. Imagine if the resolution had been no action must be taken to preempt or, if it's too late for that, to punish and to limit the damage. Which member state of the Security Council do you think would have gotten the mandate to send the heavy lifting planes and the vast supplies of medicine and relief and the forces that General Dallaire, to our shame, wasn't able to command? You know very well who would have gotten the job. Nobody can pretend otherwise.

In 1990, the first year of unified Europe, the continent takes responsibility for itself. "We don't need American patronage anymore," they say. "What's this happening on our southern borders? There appears to be genocide in Bosnia." Power has been seized by a national socialist government in Belgrade. War and racism and sectarianism are spreading like weeds all across the area. What did Europe do?

Well, the British supported the Serbs, as they always do. Everyone took the position they did in 1914. The French supported the Serbs. The Austrians supported the Slovenians. The Germans supported the Croats. The Bosnians were left orphans and would have been destroyed and the war would have spread until the point came when the European powers had to beg the United States to intervene where it did not want to, where there was no oil and no American national interest. And thanks to the U.S., the horrible bloody business was stopped. That was unilateral. The United Nations never baptized that operation. If it had been left up to Kofi Annan, Bosnia would have gone the way of Rwanda and Darfur.

What did we get in Darfur? What did we get for playing it Kofi Annan's way in Darfur? We watched another Rwanda in slow motion. No one complains about the genocide in Darfur now. Do you know why? Because it's over. It's complete. It's wrapped. All the black Muslim Africans have been destroyed or deported by the Arab Muslim fascist militia. There's nothing really to worry about, is there? We can relax. That's what you get by playing it the multilateral way.

Q: Your basic argument is that democracy is sprouting in the Middle East and that, therefore, the American invasion of Iraq is justified. However, the two aren't necessarily connected. There are many, many reasons for the sprouting of democracy in the Middle East. For example, what happened in Ethiopia had a big effect on the Middle East. What happened in South Africa also had a very powerful effect on attitudes in the Middle East. The argument could be made that the invasion of Iraq slowed down the process toward democracy. It has put into question American credentials as democrats. Obviously, an Abu Ghraib raises that question in many people's minds, "Is this just an excuse or is this for real?" I don't see that you've made the case at all that the two are connected.

A: To the question of whether or not post hoc is propter hoc in the Middle East or, in other words, are democratic developments connected or not to the coalition intervention in Iraq, those who lead these movements would not deny your analogy with South Africa or other cases. I mention the Philippines myself.

Indeed, when Saad Eddin Ibrahim was in jail in Cairo he received a very nice letter from Nelson Mandela encouraging him and adding the present of a blanket most thoughtfully. Nelson Mandela wrote and said, "I know that if you're in prison in Africa people think that it must be much too hot, but those of us who have done time in Africa know that actually the prisons are extremely cold, so you might like a blanket"—a proper fraternal gesture. The Americans believe that it was the initiative to remove, to put an end to the vile and aggressive and dangerous and unraveling maniacal regime of Saddam Hussein that actually inaugurated this sprouting of democracy.

I had a debate in London recently with a leading opponent of Tony Blair, a former Labour leader called Roy Hattersley. He's an antiwar, right-wing Labour guy. He says, "Look, the people of Lebanon rebelled because of the murder of Rafik Hariri. It had nothing to do with America in Iran." I said, "Well, now look, My Lord," because he's Lord Hattersley now, "it has been the case for twenty years that if you're a politician in Lebanon and if you criticize or you inconvenience the Syrian regime, your car blows up." We don't know if there's any connection, but those are the facts. You criticize the Syrians, your car explodes. It happened again for, I think, the tenth time in recent memory. But this time, people weren't willing to take it anymore. This time they had seen what had happened in Iraq and they had seen people voting. They had seen people celebrating in the streets at the fall of the dictatorship. It's in the highest degree unlikely that Iraq had no bearing on Lebanon.

Furthermore, the Lebanese were confronting what is now the only Baathist regime left, and I can't believe that the thought did not strike them that with Baathism dead in Baghdad it doesn't have much longer to go in Damascus.

Q: Can you shed some light on what is happening in Europe with regard to Bush, Iraq and the Middle East?

A: There's something about the personality of President Bush that doesn't travel into Canadian airspace or even Massachusetts airspace, actually. It doesn't have anything to do with the question you asked about developments in England and France, such as the bombs in London in July and the riots in the greater Paris area.

The civil war within Islam, within the Muslim world in other words, is a war between those who wish to restore the caliphate by means of jihad and impose *sharia* on all Muslims and those millions and millions and millions of Muslims who don't want to be ruled in that way, and who realize that it's an impossible, demented project using demented, suicidal means. We are caught up in their civil war because of the way we view the situation. We see the militants on the other side, the fanatics who want to win by exporting a jihad society. When we say the Muslim world, we have to bear in mind that this world now extends quite a long way into Western Europe and also into parts of North America. So when we say the Muslim world, we are not talking about the other side of the Bosporus anymore. That's obviously a very sobering reflection and one to which quite insufficient attention has been given. We're fighting for those hearts and minds, too, and against the same enemy who fancies the idea of having *sharia* in Canada. This is a rumor, I hope. I heard that it had been proposed and I thought, "No, no, no, no. Surely not."

Q: At some point the Americans are going to have to get out of Iraq, and there are some who are saying the time is now.

When do they do it? What are the circumstances under which the Americans are going to be able to get out?

A: The exit strategy is a Utopian idea. It suggests that we have learned nothing from the fact that much of this war had been and is still taking place on what we might call our own soil. It began in downtown New York and it spread to the London subway. The idea that there's "over there" and that there's "here," and we can withdraw and be here and they'd just be over there is flatly foolish. It would be like asking why the French do not have an exit strategy for the suburbs of Paris. There is no way that we can disengage. We are caught up in their civil war. We can't disengage until the right side has won that war and the other side has been conclusively, humiliatingly crushed and discredited. We didn't ask for this, but we can't pretend it hasn't happened to us.

Q (a): Can you talk a little bit about organized religion in the context of Iraq, especially given the protagonists: one is an Anglican mystic and the other is a former Anglican turned born-again. The government of Iraq has both an Islamic constitution and a strongly Shiite government. Is this a desirable result, given your remarks about Iran?

Q (b): James Fallows had an extraordinary piece in the *Atlantic Monthly* in which he says that Iraq has become terrorist central, and that with the problems of the abuse of prisoners and phosphorous bombing, which is receiving little attention in the U.S., the war is being undermined by the behavior of people on the ground. Can you comment on how this affects the exit strategy?

A: The matter of the dishonor of this great cause has kept me awake a lot. The idea that there should have been recreational sadism in Abu Ghraib, maltreatment for its own sake with not even the pretext of trying to extract information, this kind of thing is more nauseating than one is able to say. However, here is a factual statement that you will not be able to challenge.

Prison conditions everywhere in Iraq have improved beyond all recognition since the arrival of the coalition forces. That is a fact that no one can challenge. I divide people between those to whom the name Abu Ghraib is new and those who have known it for a long time. I saw Abu Ghraib. I saw what it was like when Saddam Hussein was running it. It was an abattoir. It was a mass grave. It was a center of pornography and torture on a Nurembergian scale. Iraq, at that stage, was a concentration camp above ground and a mass grave underneath it.

There is no comparison at all between the actions of the coalition forces and those of Saddam Hussein and his people. Even the delinquents among the coalition forces have been caught, exposed and arrested by officers of our armies. No comparison can seriously or morally be made even if there were some Anglicans in charge of it, and I must admit you never know with Anglicans. George Bush is actually a Methodist, like Clinton, but he joined his wife's church, probably prudently. I don't think that Mr. Blair's Anglicanism has very much to do with the war in Iraq. Certainly, the Church of

England takes the opposing view on the war with its new, completely sheep-faced archbishop, as did every Christian church of any weight, right up to the Pope's groveling to Tariq Aziz on the very eve of the intervention. I have some thoughts about those who believe themselves to be amongst us not as the result of the laws or evolution but due to a divine dispensation. I know some people think it's modest to say, "Don't mind me. God has a plan for me. I'm just, you know, fulfilling it." I don't find that modest or humble myself. I think the laws of biology explain the presence of most people whom I run into, at any rate. They seem to demonstrate evolution than otherwise.

Abba Eban was the most suave and polished of Israel's diplomats and a former British South African officer. He gave a talk in New York about the Israel-Palestine question. He was Israel's UN envoy during the 1950s and Foreign Minister from 1966–1974. I went. He said, "When you look at the Israel-Palestine question, what strikes you first, last and most of all is the absolute ease of its solution. It's the ease of its solubility." It was a brave way to start a speech.

So, what's the problem? We have two peoples of approximately equal size with perfectly justifiable claims to the same land and a long, mutual history. What is more natural than that each of them should have a state, should have a share in it? Nothing could be simpler. It would have been done a long time ago but there are some in the Zionist community who believe that God awarded them all of this land without exception and that compromise is impossible. They don't have the right to undo a divine mandate. There are many on the Muslim side who are more than willing to echo that and say their side in Jerusalem is only a part of the great future of the Muslim empire and it's all Muslim land.

Then there is the invaluable help of the Christian Zionists in Washington who say, "This looks like a promising way to bring about Armageddon and the end of days, and we must do our absolute level best to bring this about." Sometimes posing as friends of the Jews, though, they omit to say that when the final battle comes all Jews who have not converted to fundamentalist Christianity will be thrown into a pit of eternal fire. In other words, they support the Jews as the rope supports the hanging man. Religion poisons everything in this region. I don't understand how people can go around saying, "Well, religion may not be actually be metaphysically true but at least it makes people behave better." That would not be my impression. There are strong secular forces in Iraq. They are most noticeably concentrated in the Kurdish region, which refuses any mullahs or *sharia* or anything of this kind and which will not apply those provisions of the Iraqi constitution in those areas in any case, but it has to be admitted that there is a war within the war. There are people who are in favor of the liberation of Iraq who have their own religious agenda and who would ruin the whole project if it would ratify their own confession, and that has to be fought, too.

My limited experience in taking part in revolutionary combats and arguments is that you're always fighting on two fronts. It's never just, "Here is the popular front against the fascists and the plutocrats." There's always some bastard in the popular front who's working for Joseph Stalin or has ideas of his own. That's also the sign of a genuine revolution, by the way, a genuine movement that is paradoxical and dialectical. I quite like fighting on all these fronts and always, as a matter of mental hygiene, against people of faith.

A SHATTERED PACT
WITH MODERNITY

FOUAD AJAMI
FEBRUARY 7, 2006

A highly respected and articulate Middle East scholar at Johns Hopkins University, Fouad Ajami has been closely associated with the neoconservative movement that supported the U.S. invasion of Iraq. Here, he finds reasons to be optimistic about the results of America's foreign policy in the region, arguing that the incursion has given Iraqis a framework in which they can begin to wage their own war against Arab radicalism. Using the 2005 elections and the Grand Ayatollah Ali al-Sistani's moderate response to the Danish cartoon incident as examples, Ajami suggests that moderate Muslims are trying to reclaim their traditions, to take them back from the likes of bin Laden. It is an effort, he believes, that we must continue to support.

Addressing you tonight, I am reminded of a great folk character in the Arab world. It's a character named Johah. And Johah was always full of mischief. Johah was a sort of idiot savant, in many ways. And he came to an assembly one time and said—he was supposed to give a little talk—and he said, "Do you know what I am going to talk to you about?" And they said, "No." And then he said, "Well, then there is no use talking to you about anything." So he left. He came back the second time, and he said, "Do you know what I am going to talk to you about?" And they decided, well, since the answer "no" didn't work, they said, "Yes, we know." He said, "Well then, you are okay, then. I don't need to talk to you about anything." And he left. He came the third time, and he asked the same question, and half the audience raised their hands and said "yes," and half the audience said "no." And then he said, "Well, then there is no problem for me, because those of you who know can tell those of you who don't know."

There are many people here who know so much about these sad lands of the Middle East. A number of years ago my dean at Johns Hopkins University was concerned about me. He thought I was becoming somewhat irrelevant in my interests. He said, "I hear you're interested in Islam, in political turmoil in Egypt, in Anwar Sadat's assassination, and a man named Ayman Zawahiri. I think you should get on with it and modernize your concerns." I told him, "Look, I am too old to be modernized. I am just going to stick around and continue doing what I am doing." That dean was Paul Wolfowitz, by the way. As you all know, he went on to do some exciting things in the Middle East. In the end, I didn't really have to change my ways that much.

Let me try something tonight. Someone mentioned to me earlier about having nightmares regarding the current situation in the Middle East, about the anger generated by the Danish cartoons and those frightening suicide bombers. She wondered if I could say anything that would reassure her. "What can we do? What should a good 'liberal' do?" She asked if I could say something hopeful tonight.

Let me begin with the issue of Denmark, because I had come here really to talk about Iraq, because Iraq has been the obsession for me for the last three years, and Iraq has consumed much of my life, and Iraq has consumed several trips. And I am deep into a book on Iraq called *The Foreigner's Gift: The Americans, the Arabs and the Iraqis in Iraq*. So I will talk about Iraq. But before I get to Iraq, let me just say a word or two about the events in Denmark and what this really means for liberal society and what this means for Europe. Because this is really what the issue of these cartoons is all about.

Now, the template, if you will—the real analogy and the real precursor of what is happening in Denmark today—happened a generation ago, when Salman Rushdie, as you will remember, wrote *The Satanic Verses*. Here was an Indian Muslim of Bombay birth who wrote this book. And, in fact, the issues that transpired in the aftermath of *The Satanic*

Verses are exactly what we are witnessing today. With *The Satanic Verses*, the troubles began in Bradford. The troubles began in England. The book burning began in England. The activists who got hold of this issue and wanted to stay with it were in England. And Ayatollah Khomeini, when he wrote his famous "fatwa," otherwise known as his book review, you will notice that Ayatollah Khomeini came on this issue a good month or two after the events in Bradford. He happened onto it. He sensed its importance. He understood that this is really what you need to do, that this is a meaningful issue, and that if you are trying to walk away from the wreckage of the Iran-Iraq war and the defeat of Iran in this long war, or at least the frustration of Iran in this war with Iraq; if you want to give your revolutionary children, as he called them, something to think about, and if you want to situate Iran as the center of the Islamic world, then why not turn to *The Satanic Verses*. And indeed, that is exactly what happened. So the troubles began in Bradford, and then migrated to the Islamic world.

It's interesting when you think of it. You would think that Islam in Europe, what the Muslim activists call *bilad al kufr*, the lands of unbelief—I love that term. I'll come back to it. (Going to Denmark and living among the Danes, and then saying you are living in the lands of unbelief. I always correct that. I say no. It's the lands of the Danes. It's not the lands of unbelief.) So in this case you would expect that European Islam would be more tolerant, but indeed it was the other way around. And the troubles migrated from England and made their way through the Islamic world, and we saw what happened. We saw people duck for cover. We saw people either try to defend freedom of expression, or at least, in a way, take a pass on it.

Now, in the case of these cartoons, that's exactly what happened. The Muslims in Denmark, the Danish community, the activists in Denmark took their cause and took it to the Islamic world. Now, as they worked their way through the Islamic world, there was this exquisite little irony. They went into regimes which oppress Islamists, which kill Islamists, but then were more than willing to lend them a helping hand, because such is what you have to do. There was a great role played, in this crisis, by the Egyptian ambassador to Denmark. The Egyptian ambassador to Denmark became deeply engaged in this question. Now, I find that kind of ironic, that the Egyptian regime, completely secular and completely merciless in its treatment of its own Islamists, suddenly finds tremendous support, and finds that it has a lot of time and a lot of patience with the Danish activists and their concerns. Now reasonable people can disagree about whether these cartoons are pretty or not, whether they are sensible or not, whether they are in good taste or not, but the issue—the question of freedom of expression—is vital. I believe what Europe is seeing—exemplified by these cartoons—is the danger within.

Fifteen million Muslims, or even more, make their home in Europe. This demographic fact is the great story of the Islamic world today. Couple this with a declining population in Europe and put it right next to the explosive demography of the Islamic world, and you can see the dilemma of Europe. Europe is also awakening to this danger. Europe has to understand that this is not a battle between America and the Islamic world, with Europe just an innocent bystander. Europe is a battleground in this fight. Consider what has been happening in Europe. Every European country has had its kind of moment of awakening. In the case of the Danes, the cartoon incident was their moment. In the case of 7/7/2005, it was the moment of awakening for England. The kids who worked in fish and chip restaurants—how more British could you be—were then involved in deeds of terror. That was the moment of truth for Britain.

Take a look at what has happened in the case of the Dutch. Here is the most quintessentially politically correct society. It awakens to the horror with the murder of the film-maker, Theo van Gogh, when a young Dutch of Moroccan descent walked up and killed Theo van Gogh and then stuck a knife in him and left a message. During his trial he said he had no remorse. He said, "I slaughtered him." "I slaughtered him:" the language again coming from some other deep tradition and some other frightening world.

So I think, in the case of these cartoons, they really are a window into what is happening in the Islamic world, and what is happening in Europe in particular. Now, some people (Muslims?) are quick to take offense. In fact they are ready to be offended. One of the hallmarks of a liberal society, I think, is that you have to be willing to be offended. These people are not willing to be offended. They don't understand the nature of life in a modern society. As I have said many times, they are *in* the West, but they are not *of* the West. My generation of Arabs and Muslims, when we left to live and work in the West, we understood the meaning of our departure. We understood that we were leaving the failing lands of the Arab world. We accepted that bargain with separation. We understood that we couldn't take our beliefs on the road with us to foreign lands. We knew that we had to adjust to a foreign land. And even as we came out of darkness, we could see the lodestar, and the lodestar was modernity, and the lodestar meant that you just follow that path toward the modern world.

That pact with modernity, that quest for modernity, has been shattered in the Islamic world today. People ask and they say, "What does one see for the future of the Islamic world?" I really don't know. You are dealing with a world that runs all the way from Indonesia in the east to Morocco in the west. We are talking about 1.2 billion people; 20 percent of the world's population are Muslims. What can we say about them? There is enormous diversity in the Islamic world. What can you say about a religion that has the Malays and the Saudis? Not much, on some level.

But you can make a few generalizations. You can say, by and large, this population is young. Therefore Islam is young. Islam is also urban. But Muslims are also poor and poorly educated. It's not so much that they are illiterate. They are half educated. They are newly lettered. They now have access to the text so that they can read it on their own. And from the text, they can pronounce on the modern world. They can pronounce on politics. They can pronounce on my faith and yours. They can pronounce on the condition of women. They can decide for themselves and for their neighbors, and for the government, what the nature of life should be. That dilemma for the Islamic world will endure.

The question of the cartoons is just a window on the unease of modern Islam, on the inability of modern Muslims to live in their own lands where they can't really make a living. But when they move, they take the faith—and the faith has become portable today. They take it abroad and try to manipulate it, and they find themselves unable to live with others, and unable to accept the rules of the modern life. I anticipate you are going to see more of these Salman Rushdie affairs. You are going to see more of these cartoon issues flaring up.

I know that my city, the city I grew up in, Beirut, has played a part in this. We watch, if you will, the attack on the Danish Consulate in Beirut. And my little aside on attacking consulates and embassies is that these are the very same embassies that the young Muslims have to go and stand in front of and beg for visas to go to foreign lands.

Let me tell you a story. Jacques Chirac once went to Algeria, and millions of people went out into the street and they were chanting what sounded like "Vive la France." No. They were chanting in unison, one word: "visa, visa, visa." And he finally figured it out, that all the Algerians want to get the hell out of Algeria and move to France. So if you want to burn and if you want to sack these embassies and consulates, these are the very same embassies and consulates you are going to be coming to in order to find some way out of the poverty and the despair of many of these societies.

What we saw in Beirut was simple. What we saw is that the mafia in Damascus wanted to set Beirut ablaze. And these people who came and assaulted the Danish Consulate, they came into a Christian area of Beirut, Ashrafi. Beirut is divided in the old-fashioned Ottoman way. There are Christian neighborhoods and Muslim neighborhoods. And the Lebanese know better than to go into a neighborhood that is not their own. They know the rules of the road. But nevertheless, they stormed this consulate and they attacked a Maronite church in east Beirut. And when the police went and rounded up some of the suspects, we learned something about them. The largest number of people who were rounded up were Syrians. The second largest number, of course, were Palestinians. And the third, finally, bringing up the rear, were the Lebanese themselves.

If you want to really know about how cunning these regimes are, the Syrian regime orchestrating all this is hardly a pious regime. It's a regime of a minority. They themselves have had a terrible war with the Islamists in their midst. In 1982, the father of the current ruler, Hafez Assad, gunned down no less than twenty thousand people in the city of Hamma. They were principally Sunni Muslims. They were Muslim brothers who had risen against the "godless" regime of Hafez Assad. The spectacle of this very tyrannical, secular Syrian regime—considered by the pious to be ungodly and un-Islamic—suddenly awakening to this great violation that befell the Islamic world. It's a scam, and people know that it's a scam. Fortunately, I think, in this world, there are people who are now awakening to the fact that they are fouling their own nest, that they are destroying their own world. There are Islamic jurists of some moral caliber—and some substance and spine—who are trying to recover the tradition and take Islam back from these hooligans.

One of these people, I am proud to say, is none other than the Grand Ayatollah al-Sistani, the Shia leader, and a great Shia jurist in Iraq. (I could speak at length about his modesty and humble surroundings in Najaf. I could tell you about his small rented house in a tiny alleyway. But I will leave that for another time.) He has spoken with great clarity, candor and courage about the falseness of the cartoon demonstrations. These are not demonstrations of faith. They are attacks intended to give power in the Islamic world to the radicals, to the jihadists, to the extremists. The indictment by Sistani, I am proud to tell you, has meant a lot to me. I was so amazed that it actually took place.

On a recent trip to Iraq, I got to see Ayatollah Sistani. He is a very reclusive man and extremely difficult to see. Given the luck of the draw, I ended up going to Najaf and spending quite a bit of time with him. I was able to see him because of a friend of mine, as is usually the case in the Middle East: the Deputy Prime Minister of Iraq, Ahmed Chalabi. He made it possible for me to go the Grand Ayatollah Sistani. And when you see Sistani, and you see the learning of Sistani, and you see the caution of Sistani, and you see Sistani's aversion to violence and Sistani's aversion to theocracy, and Sistani's attachment to democracy itself and the ballot, you realize that the Iraqis, and the Arabs, and the region as a whole, and the Americans who came into Iraq, were fortunate that Grand Ayatollah Sistani is the way he is.

FOUAD AJAMI

Here you have this man who is Iranian by birth, comes to the Shia holy city of Najaf in his early twenties, makes his home there, lives this pious, quiet life, and is there when his country, this adopted country of his, Iraq, needs him. And if you take a look at Sistani's politics and sensibility, you can see why you can at least draw some measure of hope that the battle is joined, and that maybe some Muslims now will have to reclaim their tradition. They will have to take it back from the likes of bin Laden. They will have to take it back from the likes of these preachers in Denmark. They will have to take it back from the preachers in London. They will have to take it back from the preachers that are found throughout Europe, and all of them are on the dole. All of them enjoying the benefits of the welfare state. The welfare state sustains them. The welfare state pays them and enables them to give their sermons to mold Islam for their own purposes.

So if you want insight into the Danish cartoon affair, simply go back and review the Rushdie affair, and you'll see how similar they are —and how the whole outrage was planned and calculated.

Now onto Iraq. I have gone to Iraq many times, and I am still hopeful about that deeply troubled country. You know, I don't think you can just simply decide, well, this ride has proven to be very difficult and now I should just simply give up on Iraq and move on. That's not the morally or intellectually right thing to do. On my last trip to Iraq, I had a chance to go to Kurdistan in the northern part of the country with President Jalal Talabani. I have known Talabani for a very long time, and have to say I am very fond of him. And just as

174

the Iraqis are blessed to have Grand Ayatollah Sistani, they are blessed to have Jalal Talabani as president.

I went to Kurdistan to witness the merging together of the realms of Massoud Barzani, in one part of Kurdistan, and Jalal Talabani, in another part of Kurdistan. Looking at the Kurds and what they have made of their country after being victims of fratricide for a very long time, one sees that they have come to appreciate the gifts of democracy. You can see in Kurdistan how it has been changed, improved and reformed. You get a sense that in that part of country, American protection has afforded the Kurds a chance to build a new life.

I know there is a great controversy about the meaning of the Iraqi elections. Are they real? Are Iraqis really committed to democracy? And so on. The Iraqis have gone out now three times, and they have voted three times. They voted on January 30 [2005], and they voted for a constitution in October [2005], and they voted yet again on December 15 [2005], in a new national election. The best remark I have on the issue of this last election was that Iraq didn't really hold an election— it held a census. The Kurds went out and voted for the Kurdish list of candidates including Jalal Talabani and Massoud Barzani. In the process they elected 58 Kurdish members to the National Assembly out of a total of 275 seats.

The Sunni Arabs went out this time and defied the jihadists who traditionally target the Shia as apostates. But for political reasons, they now target Sunnis to make sure they don't go into the army, or join the police, or vote. They target the Sunni Arabs because that is the community they want to hold. This time the Sunni Arabs decided to vote, and actively participated in a free election at great risk to themselves. In the end, they sent about 60 to 70 members to the National Assembly. They have come to realize they will have to compete politically in a country they believed historically belonged to them. As of late, they believe their country was stolen from them, that the Americans came and stole it and gave it to the Kurds and the Shia. The Sunni Arabs also believe they make up a bigger share of the population than is normally attributed to them; that they are not 15 to 20 percent of the country. Every time I met a Sunni Arab leader, he would invariably tell me they make up 42 percent of the population. All Sunni Arabs I met told me the same thing. Finally, I got tired of this number and I said to them, "Look, I was raised in Lebanon. We had seventeen communities—Druze, Sunni, Shia, Greek Catholics, Greek Orthodox, Armenian Catholic, Armenian Orthodox—and each community is 42 percent of the population. So I understand that you believe Iraq is your patrimony. You believe it's a stolen country, it's war booty." This is the perception, that Iraq belongs to the conquering race, and the conquering community is the Sunni Arabs. On this point they are unreconciled. They have not come to terms with the fact that this perception of their world is finished.

Now we come to the Shia. The Shia basically competed with one big, huge slate—the United Iraqi Alliance. Grand Ayatollah Sistani, who wanted to remain politically neutral, said, "This is not my slate. Vote as you will." But the slate said, "We are the slate of Grand Ayatollah Sistani." And they were out in the streets and they knew the political game, and they were very organized. In the end they carried 128 seats in the National Assembly.

One outcome in this election which I want to flag for you was the defeat of Shia secularism. To destroy the Shia secularists was very important for the United Iraqi Alliance. For example, there is the former prime minister, Iyad Allawi. He had gotten forty seats the last time around. This time, armed with huge amounts of money—I don't know where he got it, but rumor has it from Saudi Arabia—he got only twenty-five seats. I have to admit one disappointment, and that was my friend Ahmed Chalabi, who I think is a very talented man and who will have a big future in this coming Iraqi government, didn't win a seat.

We now have this National Assembly, and we have the Iraqis trying to cobble together a national unity government. In the end, you are going to have a division of spoils in Iraq. As expected, Jalal Talabani is President, with a Kurd as Foreign Minister. And, as predicted, the Prime Minister, Maliki, is a Shia. The Minister of Interior is also a Shia because, after decades of oppression, the police force must be in their own hands. Also as I anticipated, the Minister of Defense is a Sunni. The country will be divided this way. Six or seven cabinet posts will be given to the Sunni Arabs. They insisted on it. They are going to get them, and that's fine. It could be six. It could be seven. As the American ambassador said, "As long as the bazaar is open, we are open for business." It doesn't really matter how many cabinet posts they ask for or get. At least they are competing in the political game. They now understand that the ballot and the ballot box are the ways to political power, and that's progress.

So is Iraq a success so far? Ever since this Iraq war broke out, every place I have gone, everything I have done has revolved around Iraq. People always say to me, "I read this piece that you wrote about Iraq, but what do you really think? You must have a darker conclusion about Iraq." Well, let me tell you something. I wasn't out in the street saying, "Let's do Iraq." It wasn't that kind of war. I do believe that the Iraq war was one of the two wars of 9/11. It was a September 11 war, and to the extent that you have to debate this war, you have to insist on its connection to 9/11. It is so for me. It was a war of deterrence. It was a war of deterrence against Arab radicalism. We had gone to Afghanistan. We had gone to a place that the Arabs had rented—had rented from the Taliban—but there were no targets there that were Arab. So now on to the Baathist regime in Iraq, which drew the short straw.

An example had to be made of one radical Arab regime. It couldn't have been settled in Afghanistan, so we went after the Saddam regime. And here we have this incredible project. The stakes are huge. We know that. We know that when America was defeated, or was frustrated and lost in Vietnam, East Asia circled around the Americans. It wanted to, if you will, soften the blow of their defeat, because the East Asians understood the consequences for themselves if other defeats were to follow. And they needed the protection of Pax Americana. This region, the Arab world, is very different. If America is driven out of there, the consequences would be horrendous for everyone.

So are we winning in Iraq? This is the great question. We're not losing in Iraq. And the Iraqis have come to our rescue in many ways. They have begun to take control of their own country. The political class in Iraq has begun to gel and come together. And I think this search for a national unity government will show us what this Iraq war was about. It will show us the verdict of this Iraq war. Was it expensive? Of course. Was it full of surprises? Of course. Was it full of disappointments? Of course. Did we have buyer's remorse? Of course. There is one question which I, as someone who writes history and studies history would like to ask: If the people who pulled the trigger knew what lay ahead of them, would they have pulled the trigger on March 20, 2003? I don't know the answer to this. Some them might have. Others might have hesitated. But we are there.

————

Q: Is there a likelihood of the Muslim community gaining a really preponderant political position and, if so, which state is the most likely for that to happen in, and what might be the consequences?

A: Well, I mean, I don't see it. Would they gain power in any European country? No. Are they a problem for each of these European countries we're dealing with: Denmark, Holland, France, the U.K.? Of course. And it's a security problem. It's a problem of assimilation. It's a problem of populations that don't really accept the dream and the idea of assimilation. There are people who are more alarmist about this, I mean, the idea that Muslims would come to power and so on. I don't go there. It's not that kind of challenge. It's just about this migration which refuses to play by the rules, which refuses to accept that the act of migration itself is an acknowledgment that the old world needs to be vacated. That's it—emotionally and culturally vacated. It's about the social compact of European society. And because liberal society has accepted the idea of immigration, and liberal society has accepted the canons of postmodernism, those canons will be revised. But it's not really about the takeover of power, the seizure of power. I don't see that.

Q: In light of your concerns regarding the fifth column, as it were, in England and in other European countries, would you offer some warnings about our own growing Muslim population in Canada?

A: I don't know enough about Canada. That's a good defense, you know? I don't know enough about Canada. Look, I am an immigrant. I have to assert, if you will, that migration is a fact of life. And it's not about migration. It's not about whether people have the right to leave their homelands and make new lives. It's about the rules of these whole societies. It's about the acknowledgment of modernity. It's about the recognition that if you come to a society like Canada, or a society like Holland, that you cannot say that gays should not be teaching your kids. You cannot bring the phobias of the old world into the new world. And that's really my concern. You know, migration itself is not the issue. It's that you have these preachers who have made their stand in western societies, and they have made their stand in western societies because the secular autocracies in the Arab world drove them out. You can't agitate against the Syrian regime in Damascus, but you can agitate against the Syrian regime, as did Omar Bakri, who was a famous agitator, a preacher that England finally expelled. He could come and agitate from London. That's the issue. So migration, yes. And the rights of people to pick up stakes and build new lives. I mean, that's sacred.

If you don't mind, I'll just attach a little sort of note to this. I mean, there is a young man who was at the controls of the jet, we believe, that crashed in Pennsylvania—Ziad Jarrah. He was a young Lebanese. On a clear day, I could see his village from my village. There were two schools in Beirut, which were fairly good schools. He went to one and did exceedingly well. I went to one and did very poorly, right? The difference between us was, guess what? Thirty years. I was born in 1945. He was born in 1975. And I could see the lodestar of modernity. I could see that there was a life out there that I wanted for myself. Ziad Jarrah couldn't. And that is the thing that I am looking for. What happened? What breakdown happened in the Islamic world? And what conditions in the West changed, that I came and knew I had to live by the rules and learn the rules, and Ziad Jarrah didn't? So not only was Lebanon different, but I leave you with another proposition: the West was different. People were not being asked to adhere to the new rules. My narrative is as good as your narrative. Your faith is as good as my faith. Your practices are as good as my practices.

Q: Without a tradition of democracy in Muslim countries, such as a free press, an independent judiciary and rule of law, can democracy really take root in the Middle East?

A: Well, as you might suspect, I have thought about this quite a bit—as one who started out his career by writing a book, for example, called *The Arab Predicament*, which was almost like a cultural indictment. I was giving a lecture recently in Kuwait and a man stood up and said, "Hey, Dr. Fouad, what's going on? Many years ago, you told us that this was the condition of the Arabs. Now you have come peddling this belief in democracy. Are you just carrying water for George W. Bush and Dick Cheney? Is that it? Or is it because you are stuck in Iraq and you had to come up with a new rationale for the Iraq War, and since there were no WMDs, then it became this new Wilsonianism, right?" I think it's a bit more complicated. I mean, I now believe in this democratic push in the Arab world. We have to take freedom's ride. A while ago, I was reading a history of the European revolutions of 1848—the rebellions that began in France and spread to Germany and the Italian principalities. And a quotation caught my attention. It came from an aristocrat of Piedmont, one Massimo d'Azeglio, who said, "The gift of liberty is like that of a wild horse. In some, it arouses a desire to ride. In some others, it arouses a desire to walk." Right? So some people look at a Hamas victory and say, "Aha, we had better walk, because this ride is very, very dangerous." So I really, truly sympathize with this pact, if you will, this democratic bet that President Bush has placed, and this faith that we should try democracy. And I think the speech that Bush gave to the National Endowment on Democracy on November 6, 2003, is a rare work. And I think it lays out, in a very coherent way, that for sixty years we had a pact with tyranny. We had a pact with the dictators of the Arab world. We said whatever the hell they do to their population, it's none of our business. So long as we keep the oil flowing and so long as there is stability, all will be well. So we had this pact with tyranny. And guess what? Then came the boys of 9/11, and the boys of 9/11 were children of tyranny.

9/11, if you look at it deeply, was the product of authoritarian regimes in the Arab world. So we decided, why not take this bet? Why not risk a little bit and look and think about the possibility of democracy coming to Arab lands? Now, I know the arguments against it. There are doubts about the ability, if you will, of Arab society to handle democracy. But you know, I have gone to the races on this one. I am with this democratic push. Women wanted the vote in Kuwait and secured it. Egyptians challenged the autocrat, and it didn't quite work out this way, but they will try again. The ballot came to Iraq and, believe me, it really works. People were really enthusiastic about elections.

A predicament arises, though, when someone says to you, "Better sixty years of tyranny than one day of anarchy," as if the Arab world can only handle either tyranny or anarchy, and better tyranny. And the classic strategy of Pax Americana was, "Let's do business with the autocrats." But the autocrats were brilliant, cunning, brutal, and they tricked us. What they did to their children was to say, "Hey, you can't mess with me. But if you go and hit the Americans, I'll look the other way." So yes, it's very dangerous, this freedom's ride, this horse, this wild horse. If you ride it, you may fall. But the pact with tyranny, we know what it produced.

So we have to take this gamble. I grant Bush the courage of this gamble. It's not a straight line. We're not always good. We don't always live up to our promises. We don't always support democracy. We still now have to do something, for example, about the autocrat in Cairo, who takes our coin and mocks our purposes, who has peace with Israel but absolutely peddles the worst kind of anti-Semitism and anti-modernism and anti-Americanism in his media. Still, it's worth it. So it's risky. We know the other way. We know the pact with tyranny and what the pact with tyranny has produced.

Q: How would you explain the failure of Bush and the Americans to articulate a vision of hope—that democracy is in the interests of all?

A: I disagree with you. I actually think that, to the extent that George W. Bush and the word "articulate" go together, he has articulated. There has been a doctrine about democracy which is admirable in its insistence that we cannot consign the Arab world to the old traditions of despotism. And I think if you go to the Arab world, you find enormous attachment to George W. Bush's doctrines about the spread of liberty. Talk to the Kuwaitis. Talk to many Iraqis. Our journalists are not going to tell you that Iraq is full of gratitude for America, but it is really full of gratitude. I spend an enormous amount of time with leaders and ordinary people alike, and this idea that democracy is possible has taken hold. Many Egyptians were grateful. Many Lebanese see the revolution in Lebanon. Do you think any of these people would have gone into the street to challenge Bashar Assad and Syrian armor had they not known that Bush and American power were standing nearby? Now, I realize it's not yet complete, and Syrian agents are still in Lebanon, but in fact the Lebanese owe the liberty that they have recovered to American power and to the argument that democracy is possible in Arab lands. Go back and read some of these speeches, and go back and read the statements that have been made. I think it has been a very straight-forward message that we will no longer make this bargain with autocracy.

Now, we don't always observe this. We observe this some-times in the breach. I mean, we need to worry about these two allies of ours, Egypt and Saudi Arabia. And if you go to every speech of President Bush, you will see that he is circling Egypt and Saudi Arabia. It's easy to take on the rogues. It's these regimes that are in the orbit of American power that we have to be careful with, and we are trying to nudge them in the direction of democratic reform.

I think it hearkens back to the Wilsonian idea, to the Fourteen Points that followed the Great War. Americans and Westerners may not remember this, but the twelfth point of the Fourteen Points was about the subject nations of the Ottoman Empire finding their freedom. Between Woodrow Wilson and this new campaign for democracy, we made our bed with authoritarian regimes without any scruples and any embarrassment. And now at least we have put democracy in contention. I am very appreciative of this democratic push. Hosni Mubarak now cannot run amok in Egypt. Now we know what he wants, of course. Right? He would like to bequeath power to his son. Forget liberalism, forget Marxism, it's all about "ibnism"—son of; *ibn*. So it's about ibnism. We know what Mubarak wants. He would like to bequeath power to his son. He would like to perpetuate this dynastic, despotic tradition. But we have put this democratic experi-ment in Iraq. We wanted one society in the Arab world that would show other Arabs that democracy is possible. Now, some people would say Bush chose the most difficult Arab country. Many Arabs, by the way, speak very, very pejoratively of Iraq. I want you to know that. Many Arabs think Iraq is a land destined to failure and destined to violence. Its image in Arab life is always like this. But we have made this attempt in Iraq, and we will see what will become of it.

THE NEW
ANTI-SEMITISM

BERNARD LEWIS

Bernard Lewis is internationally recognized as one of the greatest living scholars on the Middle East. He is the Cleveland E. Dodge Professor Emeritus of Near Eastern Studies at Princeton University, and the author of more than two dozen books on Middle Eastern history, including the What Went Wrong: Western Impact and Middle Eastern Response. *Lewis argues that the new anti-Semitism has gone beyond racial or religious discrimination against Jews to become both political and ideological. In a tribute to Lewis, Fouad Ajami wrote, "We travel by the light of his work. He weaves for us a web between past and present, and he can pick out, over distant horizons, storms sure to reach us before long."*

This talk is based on a lecture given by Lewis at Brandeis University on March 24, 2004, and published in The American Scholar *in 2006. Lewis spoke at the Grano Series in Toronto on May 4, 2006.*

There is a well-worn platitude that we have all heard many times before: it is perfectly legitimate to criticize the actions and policies of the state of Israel or the doctrines of Zionism without necessarily being motivated by anti-Semitism. The fact that this has been repeated ad nauseam does not detract from its truth. Not only do I accept it, but I would even take it a step further with another formulation that may perhaps evoke surprise if not shock: It is perfectly possible to hate and even to persecute Jews without necessarily being anti-Semitic.

Unfortunately, hatred and persecution are a normal part of the human experience. Taking a dislike, mild or intense, to people who are different in one way or another, by ethnicity, race, color, creed, eating habits—no matter what—is part of the normal human condition. We find it throughout recorded history, and we find it all over the world. It can sometimes be extraordinarily vicious and sometimes even amusing.

Not long after World War II, the Danes were seething with resentment against two of their neighbors: the Germans, for having occupied them, and the Swedes, for having stood by with unhelpful neutrality. A Danish saying current at the time was: What is a Swede? A German in human form. Another double-barreled insult, this one from the British army in the late 1930s, when it was concerned about two different groups of terrorists: What is an Arab? A toasted Irishman. I quote these not in any sense with approval or commendation, but as examples of the kind of really nasty prejudice that is widespread in our world.

Anti-Semitism is something quite different. It is marked by two special features. One of them is that Jews are judged by a standard different from that applied to others. We see plenty of examples of this at the present time. But there too one has to be careful. There can be different standards of judgment on other issues too, sometimes even involving Jews, without anti-Semitism or without necessarily being motivated by anti-Semitism.

For instance, in mid-September 1975 in Spain, five terrorists convicted of murdering policemen were sentenced to death. European liberal opinion was outraged that in this modern age a West European country should sentence people to death. Unheard of! There was an outcry of indignation, and strong pressures were brought to bear on the Spanish government. But in the Soviet Union and its satellite states during the same period, vastly greater numbers were being sentenced to death and executed; and, in Africa, Idi Amin was slaughtering hundreds of thousands, a large part of the population of Uganda. Hardly a murmur of protest in the Western world.

The lesson is very clear. Right-wing governments (General Francisco Franco was still in charge) are not allowed to sentence offenders to death; left-wing governments are. A further implication: slaughter of or by white people is bad; slaughter of or by people of color is normal. Similar discrepancies may be found in responses to a number of other issues, as for example the treatment of women and of ethnic or other minorities.

These examples show that even a wide disparity of standards of judgment is not necessarily in itself evidence of anti-Semitism. There may be other elements involved. For example, the comparison is sometimes made between the world reaction to the massacre of Palestinians by Lebanese Christian militiamen at Sabra and Shatila in September 1982, where some 800 people were killed, and the massacre earlier in the same year in Hama in Syria, where tens of thousands were killed. On the latter, not a dog barked. The difference, of course, was in the circumstances. In both cases the perpetrators were Arab, but in the case of Sabra and Shatila, because of the dominant Israeli military presence in the region, there was a possibility of blaming the Jews. In Hama, this possibility did not exist; therefore the mass slaughter of Arabs by Arabs went unremarked, unnoticed and unprotested. This contrast is clearly anti-Jewish. In a different way, it is also anti-Arab.

We see other instances of differing standards and methods of judgment nearer home and in a perhaps less alarming form. We hear a great deal, for example, about the Jewish lobby and the various accusations that are from time to time brought against it; that those engaged in it are somehow disloyal to the United States and are in the service of a foreign power.

The Jewish lobby is, of course, not the only lobby of its kind. Consider three others: the Irish, Greek and Armenian lobbies. The Irish lobby, which campaigned against the United Kingdom, America's closest ally, and the Greek and

Armenian lobbies, which campaigned against Turkey when Turkey was a crucial NATO ally, were seen as pursuing their legitimate concerns. I don't recall accusations against any of them of disloyalty or even of divided loyalty.

The other special feature of anti-Semitism, which is much more important than differing standards of judgment, is the accusation against Jews of cosmic evil. Complaints against people of other groups rarely include it. This accusation of cosmic, satanic evil attributed to Jews, in various parts of the world and in various forms, is what has come to be known in modern times as anti-Semitism.

In the Western world, anti-Semitism has gone through three clearly distinct phases. Some people have written and spoken about anti-Semitism in antiquity, but the term in that context is misleading. We do indeed find texts in the ancient world attacking and denouncing Jews, sometimes quite viciously, but we also find nasty remarks about Syrians, Egyptians, Greeks, Persians and the rest. There is no great difference between the anti-Jewish remarks and the ethnic and religious prejudices expressed against other peoples, and on the whole the ones against Jews are not the most vicious. The Syrian-born Roman historian Ammianus Marcellinus, for example, speaking of the Saracens, remarks that they are not to be desired either as friends or as enemies. I don't recall, in the ancient world, anything said about the Jews quite as nasty as that.

Polytheism was essentially tolerant, each group worshiping its own god or gods, offering no objection to the worship of others. Indeed, one might have been willing to offer at least a pinch of incense to some alien god, in courtesy as a visitor or, even at home, in deference to a suzerain. Only the Jews in the ancient world insisted—absurdly, according to the prevailing view of the time—that theirs was the only god and that the others did not exist. This gave rise to problems with their neighbors and their various imperial masters, notably the Romans. It sometimes provoked hostile comments and even persecution, but not the kind of demonization that has come to be known as anti-Semitism. The tendency was rather to ridicule the Jews for their faceless, formless god in the clouds and for such absurd and barbarous customs as circumcision, the rejection of pig meat and, most absurd of all, the Sabbath. Several Greek and Roman authors noted that because of this comic practice the Jews were wasting one-seventh of their lives.

Demonization, as distinct from common or garden-variety prejudice or hostility, began with the advent of Christianity and the special role assigned to the Jews in the crucifixion of Christ as related in the Gospels. Christianity started as a movement within Judaism, and the conflict between Christians and Jews had that special bitterness that often makes conflicts within religions more deadly than those between religions. The Christian message was presented as the fulfillment of God's promises to the Jews, written in what Christians called the Old Testament. The rejection of that message by the Jewish custodians of the Old Testament was especially wounding.

An important concern of the early Christians was not so much to blame the Jews as, for understandable reasons, to exculpate the Romans. Jewish guilt and Roman innocence, the two interdependent, became important parts of the Christian message, first to Rome and then beyond, with devastating effect on popular attitudes toward Jews, especially at Easter time.

For many centuries, hatred and persecution of Jews, and the ideology and terminology used to express them, were grounded in religion. Then came the phase when religious prejudice was discredited, seen as not in accord with the ideas of the Enlightenment. It was seen as bigoted; worse, as old-fashioned, out-of-date. That meant new reasons were needed for hating Jews. They were found.

The process of change began in Spain when large numbers of Jews—and also Muslims—were forcibly converted to Christianity. With a forcible conversion there was inevitably some doubt, especially among the enforcers, as to the sincerity of the converts. And this doubt was well grounded, as we know from the phenomenon of the Marranos and the Moriscos, the sometimes dubious converts from Judaism and Islam. Thus the practice arose of examining the racial origins of the so-called new Christians. We even find statutes in sixteenth-century Spain about purity of blood, *la limpieza de sangre*. Only people who could prove Christian descent for a specified number of generations could be accepted as genuine Christians. "Purity of blood" was required for certain positions and certain offices.

This is where the racial form of anti-Semitism began. It was systematized in Germany in the nineteenth century, when for the first time the term "anti-Semitism" was invented and adopted.

"Semitic" was first used as a linguistic, not as an ethnic or racial term. Like "Aryan," it was coined by philologists to designate a group of related languages. Aryan included languages as diverse as Sanskrit, Persian and, by extension, Greek, Latin and most of the languages of Europe. Semitic, similarly, brought together Syriac, Arabic, Hebrew and Ethiopic. Already in 1872 the great German philologist Max Müller pointed out that "Aryan" and "Semitic" were philological, not ethnological terms and that to speak of an Aryan or Semitic race was as absurd as to speak of a dolichocephalic (long-headed) language. "What misunderstandings, what controversies would arise," he said, from confusing the two— a correct if understated prediction.

Despite these warnings, "Semitic" was transferred from its original linguistic meaning to a new racial meaning and became the basis for a new and different bigotry. The people who advocated this bigotry spurned religious prejudice because they saw themselves as modern and scientific. Their hostility to Jews, they claimed, was based on observed and documented racial otherness and inferiority.

And then, just as religious hostility was spurned by the Enlightenment and replaced by modern and "scientific" racial hostility, so racial hostility was discredited by the Third Reich and its crimes, by the revelations after its fall of the appalling things that it had done. This discrediting of racism left a vacancy, an aching void.

This is where the third phase of anti-Semitism arises, which for want of a better term we might call political-cum-ideological Judeophobia. Race? Oh no, we wouldn't have anything to do with that. Religious prejudice? Oh no, we're far beyond that. This is political and ideological, and it provides a socially and intellectually acceptable modern disguise for sentiments that go back some two thousand years.

Turning from the Christian to the Islamic world, we find a very different history. If we look at the considerable literature available about the position of Jews in the Islamic world, we find two well-established myths. One is the story of a golden age of equality, of mutual respect and cooperation, especially but not exclusively in Moorish Spain; the other is of "dhimmi"-tude, of subservience and persecution and ill treatment. Both are myths. Like many myths, both contain significant elements of truth, and the historic truth is in its usual place, somewhere in the middle between the extremes.

There are certain important differences between the treatment, the position, the perception of Jews in the pre-modern Islamic world and in the pre-modern and also modern Christian worlds.

The story of a golden age of complete equality is, of course, nonsense. No such thing was possible or even conceivable. Indeed, among Christians and Muslims alike, giving equal rights or, more precisely, equal opportunities to unbelievers would have been seen not as a merit but as a dereliction of duty. But until fairly modern times there was a much higher degree of tolerance in most of the Islamic lands than prevailed in the Christian world. For centuries, in most of Europe Christians were very busy persecuting each other; in their spare time, they were persecuting Jews and expelling Muslims—all at a time when, in the Ottoman Empire and some other Islamic states, Jews and several varieties of Christians were living side by side fairly freely and comfortably.

The comparison has often been made between the Cold War of the twentieth century and the confrontation between Christendom and Islam in the fifteenth, sixteenth and seventeenth centuries. In many ways the comparison is a good one. But one has to remember that in the confrontation between Christendom and Islam, the movement of refugees, of those who, in Lenin's famous phrase, "voted with their feet," was overwhelmingly from west to east not from east to west.

This was tolerance and no more than that. Tolerance is by modern standards an essentially intolerant idea. Tolerance means that I am in charge. I will allow you some, though not all of the rights and privileges that I enjoy, provided that you behave yourself according to rules that I will lay down and enforce. That seems a fair definition of tolerance as usually understood and applied. It is, of course, an intolerant idea, but it is a lot better than intolerance as such, and the limited but substantial tolerance accorded to Jews and other non-Muslim communities in the Muslim states until early modern times was certainly vastly better than anything that was available in Christendom.

Prejudices existed in the Islamic world, as did occasional hostility, but not what could be called anti-Semitism, for there was no attribution of cosmic evil. And on the whole, Jews fared better under Muslim rule than Christians did. This is the reverse of what one might expect. In the canonical history, in the Quran and the biography of the Prophet, Jews come out badly. The Prophet had more encounters with Jews than with Christians, so we find more negative statements about Jews than about Christians. The biography of the Prophet records armed clashes with Jews, and in those encounters it was the Jews who were killed. Muslims could therefore afford a more relaxed attitude toward Jews in the ensuing generations.

The other advantage for Jews was that they were not seen as dangerous. Christianity was recognized as a rival world religion and a competitor in the cosmic struggle to bring enlightenment (and with it, inevitably, domination) to all humanity. This cosmic competition had important consequences. Local Christians were dangerous in that they were a potential fifth column for the Christian powers of Europe, the main adversary of the Islamic world. Jews were not suspected of being pro-Christian. On the contrary, they were seen as being reliable and even useful. It was not merely tolerance or goodwill—though these were essential preconditions—that led the Ottoman sultans to admit so many Jewish refugees from Spain, Portugal, Italy and elsewhere. Jews, especially those of European origin, were active in trade and industry, and from many documents in the Ottoman archives it is clear that they were valued as a revenue-producing asset. They were not just permitted; they were encouraged and even on a few occasions compelled to settle in Ottoman lands, especially in newly conquered provinces.

Obviously, this is not equality, but it is not anti-Semitism in any sense of the word either. The Ottomans' treatment of the Jews even included a kind of respect. We do of course find expressions of prejudice against the Jews, as against any group of people that are different, but their general attitude was of amused, tolerant superiority.

An interesting difference in hostile stereotypes can be found in anecdotes, jokes and the like. The main negative quality attributed to Jews in Turkish and Arab folklore was that they were cowardly and unmilitary—very contemptible qualities in a martial society. A late Ottoman joke may serve to illustrate this. The story is that in 1912, at the time of the Balkan war, when there was an acute threat to the Ottoman Empire in its final stages, the Jews, full of patriotic ardor, decided that they, too, wanted to serve in the defense of their country, so they asked permission to form a special volunteer brigade. Permission was given, and officers and NCOS were sent to train and equip them. Once the Jewish volunteer brigade was armed, equipped and trained, ready to leave for the front, they sent a message asking if they could have a police escort, because there were reports of bandits on the road.

This is a very interesting human document. Is it hostile? Not really. It shows a sort of amused tolerance, at once good-humored and contemptuous, that may help us to understand the bewilderment and horror at the Israeli victories in 1948 and after. We have some vivid descriptions at the time of the expectations and reactions of 1948. Azzam Pasha, who was then the secretary-general of the Arab League, is quoted as having said: "This will be like the Mongol invasions. We will utterly destroy them. We will sweep them into the sea." The expectation was that it would be quick and easy. There would be no problem at all dealing with half a million Jews.

It was then an appalling shock when five Arab armies were defeated by half a million Jews with very limited weaponry. It remains shameful, humiliating. This was mentioned at the time and has been ever since. One writer said: "It was bad enough to be conquered and occupied by the mighty empires of the West, the British Empire, the French Empire, but to suffer this fate at the hands of a few hundred thousand Jews was intolerable."

The Western form of anti-Semitism—the cosmic, satanic version of Jew hatred—provided solace to wounded feelings. It came to the Middle East in several stages. The first stage was almost entirely Christian, brought by European missionaries and diplomats. Its impact was principally on the local Christian minorities, where we find occasional recurrences of the previously little-known blood libel. In the fifteenth and sixteenth centuries this had indeed been explicitly rejected in orders issued by Ottoman sultans. It was now revived on a massive scale. The first major case was the Damascus blood libel in 1840. This kind of anti-Semitism continued to grow, at first on a small scale, during the nineteenth and early twentieth centuries, with a limited response. At the time of the Dreyfus Affair in France, Muslim opinion was divided, some against Dreyfus, some supporting him. A prominent Muslim thinker of the time, the Egyptian Rashid Rida, wrote defending Dreyfus and attacking his persecutors, accusing them not of fanaticism, since they had no real religious beliefs, but of prejudice and envy. Despite this response, one consequence of the affair was the first translation into Arabic of a batch of European anti-Semitic writings.

Then came the Third Reich, with connections to the Arab world and, later, to other Muslim countries. Now that the German archives are open, we know that within weeks of Hitler's coming to power in 1933, the Grand Mufti of Jerusalem got in touch with the German consul general in Jerusalem, Doctor Heinrich Wolff, and offered his services. It is interesting that the common image of the Germans pursuing the Arabs is the reverse of what happened. The Arabs were pursuing the Germans, and the Germans were very reluctant to get involved. Dr. Wolff recommended, and his government agreed, that as long as there was any hope of making a deal with the British Empire and establishing a kind of Aryan-Nordic axis in the West, it would be pointless to antagonize the British by supporting the Arabs.

But then things gradually changed, particularly after the Munich Conference in 1938. That was the turning point, when the German government finally decided that there was no deal to be made with Britain, no Aryan axis. Then the Germans turned their attention more seriously to the Arabs, responding at last to their approaches, and from then on the relationship developed very swiftly.

In 1940 the French surrender gave the Nazis new opportunities for action in the Arab world. In Vichy-controlled Syria they were able for a while to establish an intelligence and propaganda base in the heart of the Arab East. From Syria they extended their activities to Iraq, where they helped to establish a pro-Nazi regime headed by Rashid Ali al-Gailani. This was overthrown by the British, and Rashid Ali went to join his friend the Grand Mufti of Jerusalem in Berlin, where he remained as Hitler's guest until the end of the war. In the last days of Rashid Ali's regime, on the first and second of June 1941, soldiers and civilians launched murderous attacks on the ancient Jewish community in Baghdad. This was followed by a series of such attacks in other Arab cities, both in the Middle East and in North Africa.

While in Berlin, Rashid Ali was apparently disquieted by the language and, more especially, the terminology of anti-Semitism. His concerns were authoritatively removed in an exchange of letters with an official spokesman of the German Nazi Party. In answer to a question from Rashid Ali as to whether anti-Semitism was also directed against Arabs, because they were part of the Semitic family, Professor Walter Gross, director of the Race Policy Office of the Nazi Party, explained with great emphasis, in a letter dated October 17, 1942, that this was not the case and that anti-Semitism was concerned wholly and exclusively with Jews. On the contrary, he observed, the Nazis had always shown sympathy and support for the Arab cause against the Jews. In the course of his letter, he even remarked that the expression "anti-Semitism, which has been used for decades in Europe by the anti-Jewish movement, was incorrect since this movement was directed exclusively against Jewry, and not against other peoples who speak a Semitic language."

This apparently caused some concern in Nazi circles, and a little later a committee was formed that suggested that the Führer's speeches and his book *Mein Kampf* should be revised to adopt the term "anti-Jewish" instead of "anti-Semitic" so as not to offend "our Arab friends." The Führer did not agree, and this proposal was not accepted. There was still no great problem in German-Arab relations before, during and even for a while after the war.

The Nazi propaganda impact was immense. We see it in Arabic memoirs of the period, and of course in the foundation of the Baath Party. We use the word "party" in speaking of the Baath in the same sense in which one speaks of the Fascist, Nazi or Communist parties—not a party in the Western sense, an organization for seeking votes and winning elections, but a party as part of the apparatus of government, particularly concerned with indoctrination and repression. And anti-Semitism, European-style, became a very important part of that indoctrination. The basis was there. A certain amount of translated literature was there. It became much more important after the events of 1948, when the humiliated Arabs drew comfort from the doctrine of the Jews as a source of cosmic evil. This continued and grew with subsequent Arab defeats, particularly after the ultimate humiliation of the 1967 war, which Israel won in less than a week.

The growth of European-style anti-Semitism in the Arab world derived in the main from this feeling of humiliation and the need therefore to ascribe to the Jews a role very different from their traditional role in Arab folklore and much closer to that of the anti-Semitic prototypes. By now the familiar themes of European anti-Semitism—the blood libel, the protocols of Zion, the international Jewish conspiracy and the rest—have become standard fare in much of the Arab world, in the schoolroom, the pulpit, the media and even on the Internet. It is bitterly ironic that these themes have been adopted by previously immune Muslims precisely at a time when in Europe they have become an embarrassment even to anti-Semites.

What encouraged this development was what one can only describe as the acquiescence of the United Nations and, apparently, of enlightened opinion in the Western world. Let me cite some examples. On November 29, 1947, the General Assembly of the United Nations adopted the famous resolution calling for the division of Palestine into a Jewish state, an Arab state and an international zone of Jerusalem. The United Nations passed this resolution without making any provision for its enforcement. Just over two weeks later, at a public meeting on December 17, the Arab League adopted a resolution totally rejecting this UN resolution, declaring that they would use all means at their disposal, including armed intervention, to nullify it—an open challenge to the United Nations that was and remains unanswered. No attempt was made to respond, no attempt to prevent the armed intervention that the Arab League promptly launched.

The United Nations' handling of the 1948 war and the resulting problems shows some curious disparities—for example, on the question of refugees. At the end of the initial struggle in Palestine, part of the country was under the rule of the newly created Jewish state, part under the rule of neighboring Arab governments. A significant number of Arabs remained in the territories under Jewish rule. It was taken then as axiomatic, and has never been challenged since, that no Jews could remain in the areas of Palestine under Arab rule, so that as well as Arab refugees from the Jewish-controlled areas, there were Jewish refugees from the Arab-controlled areas of mandatory Palestine; not just settlers, but old, established groups, notably the ancient Jewish community in East Jerusalem, which was totally evicted and its monuments desecrated or destroyed. The United Nations seemed to have no problem with this; nor did international public opinion. When Jews were driven out, no provision was made for them, no help offered, no protest made. This surely sent a very clear message to the Arab world, a less clear message to the Jews.

Jewish refugees came not only from those parts of Palestine that were under Arab rule, but also from Arab countries, where the Jewish communities either fled or were driven out, in numbers roughly equal to those of the Arab refugees from Israel. Again, the response of the United Nations to the two groups of refugees was very different. For Arab refugees in Palestine, very elaborate arrangements were made and very extensive financing provided. This contrasts not only with the treatment of Jews from Arab countries, but with the treatment of all the other refugees at the time. The partition of Palestine in 1948 was a trivial affair compared with the partition of India in the previous year, which resulted in millions of refugees—Hindus who fled or were driven from Pakistan into India, and Muslims who fled or were driven from India into Pakistan. This occurred entirely without any help from the United Nations, and perhaps for that reason the refugees were all resettled. One could go back a little further and talk about the millions of refugees in Central and Eastern Europe—Poles fleeing from the Eastern

Polish areas annexed to the Soviet Union and Germans fleeing from the East German areas annexed to Poland. Millions
of them, of both nationalities, were left entirely to their own
people and their own resources.

Some other measures adopted at the time may be worth
noting. All the Arab governments involved announced two
things. First, they would not recognize Israel. They were enti-
tled to do that. Second, they would not admit Israelis of any
religion to their territories, which meant that not only Israeli
Jews but also Israeli Muslims and Christians were not allowed
into East Jerusalem. Catholic and Protestant Christians were
permitted to enter once a year on Christmas Day for a few
hours, but otherwise there was no admittance to the holy
places in Jerusalem for Jews or Christians. Worse than that,
Muslims in Israel were unable to go on the pilgrimage to
Mecca and Medina. For Christians, pilgrimage is optional. For
Muslims it is a basic obligation of the faith. A Muslim is
required to go on pilgrimage to Mecca and Medina at least
once in a lifetime. The Saudi government of the time ruled
that Muslims who were Israeli citizens could not go. Some
years later, they modified this rule.

At the same time, virtually all the Arab governments
announced that they would not give visas to Jews of any
nationality. This was not furtive—it was public, proclaimed
on the visa forms and in the tourist literature. They made it
quite clear that people of the Jewish religion, no matter what
their citizenship, would not be given visas or be permitted to
enter any independent Arab country. Again, not a word of
protest from anywhere. One can imagine the outrage if Israel

had announced that it would not give visas to Muslims, still more if the United States were to do so. As directed against Jews, this ban was seen as perfectly natural and normal. In some countries it continues to this day, although in practice most Arab countries have given it up.

Neither the United Nations nor the public protested any of this in any way, so it is hardly surprising that Arab governments concluded that they had license for this sort of action and worse. One other example: unlike the other Arab countries, the Jordanians were at that time willing to accept Palestinian refugees as citizens, and the Jordanian nationality law of February 4, 1954, offered Jordanian citizenship to Palestinians, defined as natives and residents of the mandated territory of Palestine—"except Jews." This was clearly stated. Not a murmur of protest from anyone, anywhere.

These examples may serve to illustrate the atmosphere within which the new Arab anti-Semitism grew and flourished. After the 1967 war, the Israelis came into possession of the former Arab-occupied Palestinian territories, including a number of schools run by UNRWA, the United Nations Relief and Works Agency. These schools were funded by the United Nations. When the Israelis had a chance to look at the Syrian, Jordanian or Egyptian textbooks that these UN-funded schools used, they found many examples of unequivocal anti-Semitism. Although the Israelis could do nothing about anti-Semitism in textbooks in Arab countries, they felt that they could do something about anti-Semitism in textbooks used in schools funded and maintained by the United Nations. The matter was referred to the UN, which referred it to UNESCO, which appointed a commission of three professors of Arabic—one Turkish, one French and one American. These professors examined the textbooks and wrote a lengthy report saying that some textbooks were acceptable, some were beyond repair and should be abandoned, and some should be corrected. The report was presented to UNESCO on April 4, 1969. It was not published.

For those who needed it, all this provided an up-to-date, intellectually and socially acceptable rationale for what ought to be called anti-Semitism but, since that word isn't acceptable, might be called Jew-baiting, Jew-hating or generally being unpleasant to Jews. The rationale has thus served two purposes—one for Jews, the other for their enemies. In anti-Semitism's first stage, when the hostility was based in religion and expressed in religious terms, the Jew always had the option of changing sides. During the medieval and early modern periods, Jews persecuted by Christians could convert. Not only could they escape the persecution; they could join the persecutors if they so wished, and some indeed rose to high rank in the church and in the Inquisition. Racial anti-Semitism removed that option. The present-day ideological anti-Semitism has restored it, and now as in the Middle Ages, there seem to be some who are willing to avail themselves of this option.

For non-Jews the rationale brought a different kind of relief. For more than half a century, any discussion of Jews and their problems has been overshadowed by the grim memories of the crimes of the Nazis and of the complicity, acquiescence or indifference of so many others. But inevitably, the memory of those days is fading, and now Israel and its problems afford an opportunity to relinquish the unfamiliar and uncomfortable posture of guilt and contrition and to resume the more familiar and more comfortable position of stern reproof from an attitude of moral superiority. It is not surprising that this opportunity is widely welcomed and utilized.

The new anti-Semitism has little or no bearing on the rights and wrongs of the Palestine conflict, but it must surely have some effect on perceptions of the problem, and therefore on the behavior and perhaps even on the policies of both participants and outsiders. Nor is the offense all on one side. One might argue that when Arabs are judged by a lower standard than Jews, as for example the minimal attention given to the atrocious crimes committed at Darfur, this is more offensive to Arabs than to Jews. Contempt is indeed more demeaning than hatred. But it is less dangerous.

ABOUT THE
CONTRIBUTORS

WILLIAM KRISTOL

William Kristol, one of America's leading political analysts and media commentators, is editor of the influential Washington-based political magazine, the *Weekly Standard*. Prior to starting the *Weekly Standard*, he led the Project for the Republican Future, where he helped shape the strategy that produced the 1994 Republican congressional victory. Before coming to Washington in 1985, Mr. Kristol taught politics at the University of Pennsylvania and Harvard's Kennedy School of Government. More recently, he co-authored the bestselling *The War Over Iraq: Saddam's Tyranny and America's Mission*.

MICHAEL IGNATIEFF

Michael Ignatieff is an internationally known writer and broadcaster. His award-winning television series, "Blood and Belonging: Journeys into the New Nationalism," examined the issue of nationalism in the late twentieth century. He has written a number of books including *The Warrior's Honour: Ethnic War and the Modern Conscience* and *Virtual War: Kosovo and Beyond*. His most recent book, *Lesser Evil: Political Ethics in an "Age of Terror,"* examines the tensions between the values of liberal democracies and waging war against terrorism. At the time of his lecture, Mr. Ignatieff was Carr Professor and

Director of the Carr Center for Human Rights Policy at Harvard University. A front-runner in the recent race for leadership of Canada's Liberal Party, Ignatieff now serves as a member of parliament.

SAMUEL P. HUNTINGTON

Samuel P. Huntington is one of the most influential political scientists of his generation. He is the Albert J. Weatherhead III University Professor at Harvard University, where he is also Director of the John M. Olin Institute for Strategic Studies and Chairman of the Harvard Academy for International and Area Studies at the Center for International Affairs. Dr. Huntington is the author of over a dozen books including *The Clash of Civilizations and the Remaking of World Order*, which Zbigniew Brzezinski described as a "tour de force that will revolutionize our understanding of international affairs." The book has been translated into twenty-two languages.

JOHN LUKACS

Described by Jacques Barzun as "...one of the outstanding historians of the generation and, indeed, of our time," John Lukacs has been praised by critics as a historian who has the literary talents of a novelist. He is the author of more than twenty books, including *Outgrowing Democracy: An Historical Interpretation of the U.S in the 20th Century*, *The Hitler of History*, and the bestselling *Five Days in London: May 1940*. A recipient of the Ingersoll Prize, Professor Lukacs served from 1947–94 as professor of history at Chestnut Hill College, and also served as a visiting professor at many universities, including Columbia, Princeton, Johns Hopkins University and at the University of Budapest in his native Hungary.

ROBERT KAPLAN

Robert Kaplan is the highly acclaimed author of seven books on international affairs and the Middle East, including *Balkan Ghosts*, *The Arabists*, *The Ends of the Earth* and *The Coming Anarchy*. His recent book, *Eastward to Tartary*, takes readers on a geopolitical tour of the Middle East, the Balkans and the Caucasus. Mr. Kaplan is also an accomplished essayist, having published numerous cover stories in the *Atlantic Monthly*, the *New York Times*, the *Wall Street Journal* and the *Washington Post*.

CHRISTOPHER HITCHENS

Christopher Hitchens is perhaps the most brilliant and controversial political commentator and essayist in America today. A prolific writer, he is the author of more than ten books including, most recently, *A Long Short War: The Postponed Liberation of Iraq*, *Why Orwell Matters*, *The Trial of Henry Kissinger* and *Letters to a Young Contrarian*. He is currently a contributing editor to *Vanity Fair*, and writes regularly on various topics for *Harper's*, the *Los Angeles Times Book Review*, *Slate*, the *New York Times* and the *Washington Post*.

FOUAD AJAMI

Fouad Ajami is the Majid Khadduri Professor and Director of Middle East Studies at the Johns Hopkins University School for Advanced International Studies in Washington, D.C. He is the author of *The Dream Palace of the Arabs: A Generation's Odyssey*, *The Arab Predicament*, *Beirut: The City of Regrets*, *The Vanished Imam* and other works. His essays have appeared in the *New Republic*, the *New York Times Book Review*, the *Times Literary Supplement* (London), the *Wall Street Journal*, the *Washington Post Book World* and the *New York Times*.

BERNARD LEWIS

Bernard Lewis is the Cleveland E. Lodge Professor Emeritus of Near Eastern Studies at Princeton University. He is internationally recognized as one of the greatest living scholars of the Middle East. Some of his many books include *The Middle East: A Brief History of the Last 2,000 Years*, *The Emergence of Modern Turkey*, *The Arabs in History* and the international bestseller, *What Went Wrong? Western Impact and Middle Eastern Response*. Since 9/11 Professor Lewis has been an advisor to the President on Middle Eastern affairs.

ABOUT THE
EDITORS

PATRICK LUCIANI

Patrick Luciani is co-director of the Salon Speakers Series. His background is in economics and public policy. He has headed a major public policy foundation in Canada, worked as an economist and freelance writer, and is a bestselling author. He is currently a Member at Massey College, University of Toronto, and Senior Fellow on Urban Affairs at the Atlantic Institute for Market Studies. Luciani holds a Masters degree from the John F. Kennedy School of Government at Harvard University.

RUDYARD GRIFFITHS

Rudyard Griffiths is co-director of the Salon Speakers Series. Griffiths is also the co-founder of the Canadian think tank The Dominion Institute and is an advisor to the Woodrow Wilson Center in Washington, D.C. Griffiths writes a regular column on Canadian issues and international affairs for Canada's highest-circulation paper, *The Toronto Star*. He has edited various books on Canadian history and politics. Griffiths serves on the boards of the Stratford Festival and Adrienne Clarkson's Canadian Institute for Citizenship. In 2006, he was recognized as one of Canada's Top 40 under 40. He is a graduate of Emmanuel College, Cambridge.